Macroeconomics for Managers

W. DUNCAN REEKIE
University of Edinburgh

Philip Allan

First published 1980 by

PHILIP ALLAN PUBLISHERS LIMITED
MARKET PLACE
DEDDINGTON
OXFORD OX5 4SE

0 86003 510 7 (hardback)
0 86003 610 3 (paperback)

Set by MHL Typesetting Ltd, Coventry
Printed in Great Britain at
The Camelot Press Ltd, Southampton

For Charles Baird who stimulated
my interest in attempting to analyse
economic aggregates using a micro
approach

Contents

Preface

This book is designed for managers and MBA students who are required to study some macroeconomics in a compressed period of time. Their needs are currently ill-served by the majority of locquacious textbooks. Further, such readers are frequently bewildered by the apparently endless confrontation between 'Keynesians' and 'Monetarists'. They become even more confused when they see nations such as Britain pursuing persistent policies of deficit budgeting (i.e. expenditures exceeding income) in the name of economic orthodoxy. This would not represent 'good housekeeping' in their businesses, nor in their homes. Neither does it do so at the national level.

Inflation, unemployment, the balance of payments and the foreign exchange rate, are phrases frequently on the lips of newsreaders or mentioned by the press. Governments take action to influence these variables. What do they mean and why do governments adopt the policies they do?

These questions are of more than passing interest to the manager. His domestic pricing policies will be heavily influenced by his expectations of inflation. Whether he hires men or allows 'natural wastage' to occur will depend on his forecasts of unemployment in the future. Will it be difficult or easy for him to hire extra men in a succeeding period? What price should he charge for goods in his export markets?

How will the price of imported raw materials affect his costs? Does it matter if he deals in pounds and his customers or suppliers deal in dollars?

The answers to each of these questions are clearly important. Realising this, most businesses now spend a greater or lesser amount of time assessing the health of the overall economy. They purchase macroeconomic forecasts and pore over the city pages of the daily press and the *Financial Times*. There, unless already trained in economics, they find their confusion worse confounded. Concepts such as GNP, the multiplier, deficit budgeting, tap stock, the money supply, velocity and floating exchange rates, are used with what can be baffling frequency. This book was written in part to remove the apparent mystery surrounding what can appear to outsiders as mere jargon. It emerges after several years of attempting to teach macroeconomics to MBA students, and to explain it to businessmen in and out of the university environment. These attempts were at first seldom successful. Part of the reason was no doubt my own inadequacy as an interpreter; but undoubtedly existing texts (which to time-pressed businessmen were too long to read) and the methodology of economics (which seemed to many to be more concerned with serving the self-interest of politicians or career economists rather than the general good) were also to blame.

Because of the book's emphasis and departure from much prevailing conventional thought, some chapters are relatively new to the textbook literature. In particular, Chapter 3 has been resurrected from an undeserved obscurity. It is a chapter which requires an understanding of micro not macroeconomics. As a consequence readers new to the subject have only the 'Supply and Demand' and other 'micro' sections of Chapter 1 as a foundation. These should be read carefully and only then should Chapter 3 be attempted. The remainder of the book is no more difficult than most introductory macro-texts and differs only in its emphasis on the need to study the microeconomic underpinnings of the national economy.

I owe a debt of gratitude to the work of Professor Charles Baird of California State University, whose writings and teachings on the subject have proved to me that the abstruse

and esoteric approaches of some economists can be simplified.
I also am doubly thankful to him for emphasising to me the
fallacy of much modern economic thinking. As a consequence
this book attempts to synthesise the best elements of the past
with those of the new, and tries to do so in a simple and
compressed manner. In brief, I hope the reader who masters
the book will not only be able to understand the statements
of politicians, and the economic columns of the *Financial
Times,* but will be able also critically to evaluate them.

W. Duncan Reekie
Fordell, 1979

1
Introduction

Economics can assist the manager in a variety of ways. It can provide decision-making techniques; it can increase understanding of the market environment and the exchange process; and it can provide theories and methods of analysis which, if applied to the decision situation, can help the manager tackle the problems of his firm in a rigorous and probing manner. This volume has been deliberately put together with the aim of helping the manager understand the economic environment in the broadest sense.

Man is incapable of satisfying all his wants as an individual. He must *exchange* his output for that of others. From this truth comes the basis of the modern cooperative economy and *division of labour*. Exchange takes place in the *market* and commodities traded there have a *price*. Unless the price is sufficiently low, that is unless the seller sets the price at or below the *value* placed on it by the consumer, the commodity will not be bought. Value is a *subjective* phenomenon and the consumer is soverign. This applies in all markets. Whether the commodity traded in is a final consumer good or labour; whether the buyer is a final consumer or an employer.

The difficulty facing the *entrepreneur* is that if he wishes to make a *profit* he must take decisions using the *data of the market today* with a view to satisfying the *wants of the market tomorrow*. Obviously the manager or entrepreneur who today correctly assesses tomorrow's consumer wants will make a *profit*. He who does not will make a *loss*. Entrepreneurial activity is a perpetual struggle against *time*. Even statistical probability distributions can only tell us what has happened or may have happened. They can tell us what might happen, but they cannot tell us what will happen. In a word, every business decision must be taken by intuition. Every enterprise is essentially speculative. The entrepreneur is he who bears the loss if his intuition is incorrect.

If the *state assumes the risk of the entrepreneur* it can merely pass the burden on to the public at large. As Ballvé puts it, '*What the entrepreneur cannot foresee, nobody can foresee*'.

Nevertheless, managers must plan (as entrepreneurs) and they must do so using the best available information. Just as the future is only partly determined by the past, so today's opportunities only sometimes are. To the extent that this is so the following pages can aid decision-taking. Some warn not to place overmuch reliance on past data. Still others show what the outcome may be if the entrepreneur's costs are forced by government on to the populace as a whole. Wrong decisions may be arrived at. Extra costs will be incurred and government, to disguise the fact, will resort to inflation and the monetary printing press. 'The government effectively pours water into its citizens' wine and then appropriates a share of the watered wine for itself' (Ballvé). Money is taken from some and given to others and the market data (on which decisions are based) in the labour, bond and other markets are significantly altered.

Virtually all of these and other relevant problems can only be tackled by microeconomics. Yet this book is about 'macroeconomics'. What is the difference? If there is a difference can it be reconciled or only glossed over? We will take the view that reconciliation is possible but that businessmen and other citizens must be aware of how and why.

The consumer is best served by entrepreneurs operating freely in a market unfettered by government but governed by consumers. Only then will economic welfare be maximised. Only then will firms realise fully the limits of government and gain the self-confidence, so lacking in recent years, to exploit fully their own potential, given relatively accurate price, interest and wage 'signals' in the various markets.

'MICRO' AND 'MACRO'

Two villains, nature and other people, prevent us from enjoying all we want. Economics is basically the study of methods of accommodating infinite human wants to finite resources. There are three methods a society can choose to resolve the problem of scarcity — first, the command system; second, unenforced good behaviour; and third, the market system. Benevolence does not work outside small groupings such as families or clubs. In wider groupings the incentive is missing and information as to who wants what and which methods should be used to produce which goods is inadequate. The command system also faces an information problem, but this is overcome if those who give the orders are prepared to impose their preferences on others. Only the market system provides the information necessary (prices) and the incentives (profits) to permit a system of non-coercive cooperation.

All societies use a mixture of these methods of choice — choice between what goods and services to produce, choice between present consumption and investment for growth and enhanced consumption in the future. 'Macroeconomics' is concerned with issues such as stable prices, unemployment, the government sector, growth, foreign trade, the value of sterling and income distribution. 'Microeconomics' examines consumer behaviour and firm activity and the interaction of the two in various types of market.

SCARCITY

The economic problems of 'what' to produce, 'how' to produce it and 'for whom' have been with us since Eden. The production possibility frontier highlights these problems. The curve in figure 1.1 shows society's limited production possi-

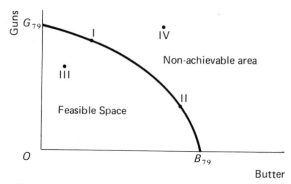

Figure 1.1

bilities. OG_{79} is the maximum possible output of guns in 1979 if all the nation's resources are devoted to manufacturing guns. Likewise, OB_{79} is the maximum possible output of butter. The curve depicts the known limits on all gun/butter combinations society can produce in 1979. For example, either of points I or II may be chosen, thus answering the 'what' question, and also the 'how' question, since only the most efficient known techniques will take the economy on to the frontier. Point IV is impossible to attain given resource scarcity and the current limits of knowledge. Point III may or may not be the result of output produced in a manner which is efficient by engineering standards (if it is, there will be unemployment in the economy) but it is certainly economically inefficient: not all resources are being fully employed in the most technologically efficient manner. The 'for whom' question is partially solved by figure 1.1 as well. For example, if point I is chosen, the recipients will be soldiers rather than civilians. Had the axes represented Fords and Rolls Royces a similar comment could have been made about the already wealthy and middle income groups. Basically, however, 'for whom' is a political, not an economic question.

OTHER USES OF THE PRODUCTION POSSIBILITY CURVE

The production possibility frontier can also illustrate the concepts of economic growth, diminishing returns, economies of scale and increasing (opportunity) costs.

If economic growth occurs the cause may be technological progress, or savings and abstinence from consumption in 1979 in order to invest in more productive capital equipment for use in a later year, or the addition of more primary factors of production (land and labour). In each case the curve is moved up, out and to the right. Point IV in figure 1.1 then may become achievable. Investment in more productive capital equipment in 1979 implies that the 1979 axes represent all current 1979 consumption (including guns and butter) and, as an alternative choice, capital equipment, which is a secondary factor of production. Capital goods are goods produced today in order to produce either more capital goods or consumer goods for use tomorrow. Division of labour results and time-consuming, indirect (but more productive) methods of manufacture are employed. Few of us make and sell a final commodity. Would any one of us even know how to make a graphite pencil?

Diminishing returns occur given constant technology and a fixed supply of all inputs but one. Say labour supply is the only varying input. The law of diminishing returns states that, given any fixed input, then as more and more units of variable input are added, after a point the extra output resulting from one extra unit of the variable input will decline. Thus in figure 1.2, if these assumptions hold but the labour supply is increased from 1 million to 2 million to 3 million respectively on curves A, B and C then the law is illustrated.

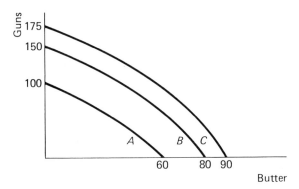

Figure 1.2

Economies of scale also occur given constant technology but variation in other assumptions. In particular, all inputs are permitted to vary. Thus if *A, B* and *C* were three economies, each of which had double the inputs of the preceding economy, then if economies of scale are present the potential output of *B* as represented by the production possibility curve would be more than double that of *A* and that of *C* more than double that of *B*.

The law of increasing (opportunity) costs explains why the production possibility frontier is curved. In figure 1.3, at points *A* or *D* to obtain 1 more unit of butter requires movement from *A* to *C* or *D* to *F*. This requires forgoing or giving up some guns (namely, *AB* guns or *DE* guns.) To acquire extra butter means a trade off or an opportunity cost must be incurred. Moreover, this cost increases as movement takes place along the curve from *A* to *D* (*AB* > *DE*). The presence of increasing costs is due to the heterogeneity of inputs in the economy. The land or other resources transferred first of all from guns to butter production will be well suited to butter but ill suited to gun manufacture. After a point, however, good gun manufacturing sites, near iron ore fields, coal mines and so on will have to be given over to dairy farming, an industry which will already be using the most fertile farming land in the country.

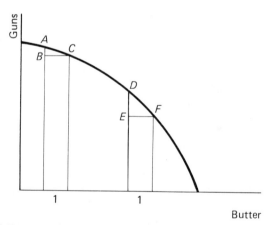

Figure 1.3

COMPETITION

Given scarcity, competition (or discrimination and choice) between people is unavoidable. Competition is a means of allocating scarce resources between persons. Competition can imply rivalry by running a race, entering a beauty competition, being or not being black or a Jew, or whatever. The winners would be allocated society's resources. This implies the survival of the fittest, the fastest runners, the most beautiful girls, or the 'best' by whatever yardstick of discrimination is employed. If, as in a market system, competition is by productivity and efficiency, then not only is personal prejudice and whim minimised, but the fittest who survive and are rewarded also push the production possibility frontier outwards to embrace previously non-attainable areas.

In a market system competition is by exchange and production of private property. As Adam Smith wrote:

> It is not from the benevolence of the butcher, the brewer, or the baker, that we expect our dinner, but from their regard to their own interest. We address ourselves not to their humanity but to their self love.

This does not exclude charity or altruism. It simply means that charity itself, like guns or butter, is a scarce commodity, and men choose between how they allocate their total (scarce and limited) efforts between charitable acts and non-charitable ones. Economics does not imply that a man is interested only in his own welfare — he is selfish, yes; but 'selfish' in economics simply means that the individual himself wants the right to make the trade-off between charitable and non-charitable options.

CHOICE AND EXCHANGE[1]

Human beings react predictably in accordance with six behavioural postulates.

---

1. The next two sections are adapted from A.A. Alchian and W.R. Allen, *University Economics*, Wadsworth 1977.

1. For everyone some goods are scarce.
2. Each person wants more than one good; so, given scarcity, choice and discrimination are necessary.
3. Each person is willing to give up some of one good to get more of another. No one continues steadfastly to refuse to give up the tiniest amount of what he possesses if he is offered sufficient in return. The smallest amount of beer a person would insist on getting to induce him to give up one packet of butter is called the marginal personal use value of a packet of butter. It is the amount of beer regarded as just equivalent in value to him of that packet of butter. It is also the largest amount of beer the other party to the trade would be willing to give up to receive one more pack of butter. Neither good has an intrinsic or built-in value. The value is not absolute or related to production inputs in any way. Value is always defined or measured in terms of a trade-off with some other good. Moreover, it is the marginal unit that matters. The totality of beer or butter owned by either party is irrelevant.
4. The more one has of any good, the lower its marginal personal use value is. This is a natural follow-on from the last point. The more one has of anything, the less valuable are the uses to which extra units may be put. Water is used for drinking, sanitation, washing, cleaning the car and watering the lawn. This explains the 'paradox of value'. Diamonds, which have a low value in use, have a high price while water, which is vital, has a low price. Yet the marginal diamond in a jewel box may well be the only one there. It is very valuable to its owner. The marginal pint of water can be poured down the sink. Economics examines marginal values not total values.
5. Not everyone has identical tastes or preferences.
6. People are innovative and rational and will try to improve their position.

These postulates can be shown on a marginal use value graph as in figure 1.4. The vertical bars show a person's marginal valuation of successive pints of beer in terms of packs of butter forgone to obtain them. Again, this emphasises that value is not simply monetary. Postulates 2 and 3 (desire for more and substitutability) state that a gain or loss of beer

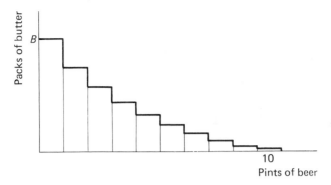

Figure 1.4

can be offset by a loss or gain of butter. Postulate 4 (diminishing marginal personal value or utility) is displayed by the downward slope of the line to the right. Postulate 1, scarcity, is depicted by the limited absolute number of pints of beer (10) he can possess *vis à vis* the maximum number of butter packs (B) he can obtain. A wealthy person would have a line located further from the origin, but its boundaries would still be finite. This indicates that a wealthier person would pay more for a unit more of beer (the height of each bar would be greater). But the amount of butter anyone would be willing to forgo to obtain one more unit of beer depends not only on the position of the line, but also on the stock of any particular good he has, namely on the position he is at on the line. Postulate 5 (differing tastes) indicates that the shapes or slopes of the lines will differ even for people of identical total wealth, although all will slope down.

Finally, before putting the postulates to use there is one further observation about human behaviour. Knowledge is imperfect and no one can foresee the future or the consequences of actions, so regrets are possible.

SUPPLY AND DEMAND

Mutually beneficial trade does not exist because people have a surplus to their requirements. It occurs (given scarcity) because people place different marginal valuations on what

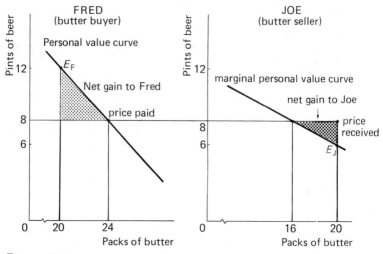

Figure 1.5

they exchange. For example, Fred puts a higher marginal value on a pack of butter than does Joe in figure 1.5 (12 pints of beer against 6) at the initial endowment points of E_F and E_J. So mutually advantageous opportunities for trade exist. Butter will be sold to Fred by Joe until Fred's marginal valuation has declined to that of Joe's. Fred values a pack of butter at 12 pints of beer and will gladly buy an extra pack at any price below 12 pints. Joe values butter at 6 pints of beer and will gladly sell a pack for any price above 6 pints. Say Joe and Fred decide to trade at a price of 8 pints of beer. Fred will buy 4 extra packs of butter worth respectively 11, 10, 9 and 8 pints of beer to him, so increasing his stock of butter to 24 packs. Joe will sell 4 packs, reducing his stock to 16. He will receive 8 pints of beer for each pack, although they were worth respectively 6½, 7, 7½ and 8 pints to him. In short, Joe will get more beer (as valued by him) than his butter is worth (to him) and Fred will get more butter (as valued by him) than his beer is worth (to him). Both will benefit by an amount equal to the shaded triangles of the diagram. Trade will have benefited both just as if there had been a magical increase in the quantity of beer. Trade is as productive (to the economist and to the participants) as is manufacture.

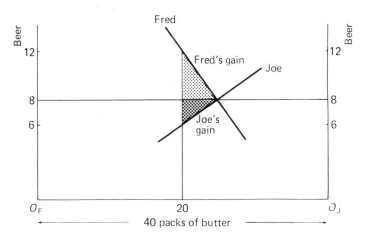

Figure 1.6

The trading continues until both have the same marginal
valuations, when no further gains from exchange are possible.
Both place the same marginal value on a pack of butter. This
can been seen more clearly if Joe's diagram is flipped over
180° from right to left and superimposed on Fred's in such a
way that the total length of the base is the total availability
of butter (40 packs). It is now easy to see (figure 1.6) that
originally Fred's marginal valuation of butter is higher than
Joe's and trading continues until they are equal. The intersection point, at a price of 8 pints of beer is obviously the
point of maximum benefit. To the left the gains from trade
are not exhausted. To the right both Joe and Fred are providing
each other with commodities they value less than what they
are acquiring. (Joe for example gives up a pack of butter for
8 pints of beer, but actually values his 15th pack of butter at
8½ pints: Fred pays 8 pints for a pack of butter but only
values his 25th pack at 7 pints.)

These marginal value lines can be regarded as demand
curves. In the flipped diagram Joe's demand curve is simply
reinterpreted as the supply curve of butter to Fred. If we
now add every individual's demand and supply curves for
butter together we obtain the market demand and supply
schedules (figure 1.7). Because barter of butter for beer is

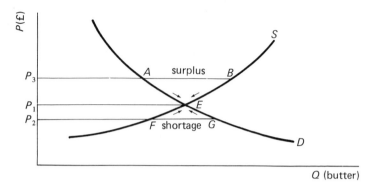

Figure 1.7

both costly and unrealistic the vertical axis is expressed in monetary units.

The demand curve slopes down, other things being equal, because more people will buy at a lower price and also existing buyers will buy more. At a lower price individuals will substitute butter for other goods such as margarine, cheese and so on. The supply curve slopes up, other things being equal, because more people will sell butter at higher prices and existing sellers will sell more. At a higher price producers will substitute butter production for other activities such as beef production. The increased real price for butter (provided it is high enough) will encourage this substitution despite the presence and operation of either of the laws of diminishing returns or increasing costs.

The point P_3 indicates a position where the price is so high there is a surplus of AB units of butter. At that price sellers will lower their prices to get rid of inventories, some sellers will then drop out of the market, and additional buyers will be attracted in. This process will continue until equilibrium is reached at E, price P_1.[1] This is called equilibrium since below

---

1. The P on the vertical axis is relative price not absolute cash price. That is, the nature of the trade-off must not be forgotten because money is being used. Thus P is not cash P, but rather cash P divided by some sort of average price for all other goods in the economy, as for example, the retail price index. Both for reasons of convention and ease we will simply label the vertical axis P, not P/RPI which would be both more correct and more meaningful.

that level, at P_2, a corresponding shortage would exist of *FG*. The low price is encouraging high consumption but low production. Unsatisfied purchasers will start bidding prices up, some buyers will drop out of the market and the higher prices encourage suppliers to increase their quantity supplied until equilibrium is again achieved.

It takes little additional thought to imagine what happens in markets where governments impose price floors of, say P_3, as with equal wage legislation; or price ceilings of, say P_2, as with the rented housing market.

If other things are not equal then the whole picture could change. For example, if tastes changed in favour of butter, if incomes increased, or the price of margarine rose, then the whole demand curve for butter would shift out to the right and a new equilibrium price would be established at a higher level (or vice versa if the reverse occured).

Equally, if supply increases, at each and every price more will be supplied. The curve will move down and to the right. This could occur because of technological changes lowering production costs, good seasons for dairy cattle breeding or falls in the costs of animal feedstuffs. (Again the supply curve would rise up and to the left under the opposite circumstances.)

'MACRO' – MARKETS

In macroeconomics proper, individual markets (such as that for butter) are not examined. Only four markets are analysed. These are the commodity, labour, money and bond markets.

In the commodity market all goods and services produced in the economy are added together into a single commodity or composite good. Supply and demand for that good are called aggregate supply and aggregate demand respectively. The price of this composite good can be thought of as the average of the millions of money prices of the millions of goods which go to make it up.

Similarly, all of the diverse types and qualities of labour services (teachers, civil servants, dustmen, engineers, scientists, hair dressers, computer analysts, surgeons) are lumped together into the single composite labour market. Again, the price of labour is the average of all the differing wages or salaries actually paid in the market.

The money market includes cash in circulation and bank balances against which cheques can be written (current accounts) and the bond market consists of all financial assets other than those defined as money. All of these (stocks, bills, bonds, shares, building society accounts, etc.) are aggregated into one imaginary bond on which there is an interest payable which, in macroeconomics, is 'the' rate of interest.

The only justification for aggregating in this way is by asking if the outcome is meaningful. Apples, after all, cannot be added to oranges. Whether or not the answer is in the affirmative the reader can judge for himself in the following pages.

2
National Income

National income data are the figures which tell us how much
an economy produces in any given period or year. They make
possible (with significant reservations) economic comparisons
between years and between countries. Gross national product
(or GNP) can be defined and measured in two alternative
ways: the expenditure approach measures the sum of the
monetary outlays made in a year when all final goods and
services in the economy are purchased. The income approach
is the total monetary value of all the final goods and services
produced in the economy.

The two methods of measuring GNP provide the same
result and can be represented in a simple flow diagram (thus
excluding government and foreign trade) as in figure 2.1.

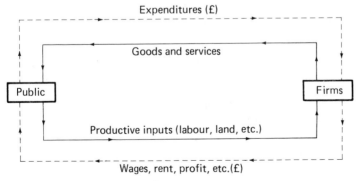

Figure 2.1

THE EXPENDITURE APPROACH

Total expenditure falls into four main categories: consumer expenditure (C), investment (I), government expenditure (G) and net exports $(X - M)$, or exports less imports. Here the definitions employed by government statisticians will be detailed.

Consumption by final consumers includes all spending on newly produced goods and services excluding only newly constructed houses. A second-hand car sale, for example, would not be included since it would not have been produced in the period under study and should not, therefore, be counted. Similarly, household savings are not included (e.g. purchases of stocks or shares, or the placing of money in deposit accounts).

Investment expenditure includes purchases by households of new dwellings, but it refers mainly to the purchase of new factory buildings, new plant and new equipment by firms (not second-hand purchases). It also includes net additions to stocks or work in progress. This inclusion must be made if the two measures of GNP are to equal each other. Since the act of production for stock gives rise to incomes whether or not the stock is sold in the current period, then the incomes will be included in the lower loop of the diagram (the income approach to GNP measurment). If the upper loop (the expenditure approach) is to maintain its identity with the lower loop then inventory increases or decreases must be included in expenditure. They are counted as net investment or disinvestment, whether planned as such or not by the actual person or firm making the investment.

Government expenditure includes both capital expenditure and expenditures on goods and services for final consumption (military equipment, hospitals, roads, fire appliances, civil servants' salaries, red tape, etc.). Transfer payments are excluded, however. These are payments made by government by taking money from one section of society and redistributing it to another (old age pensions, social security payments, student grants, etc.). All that has happened here is that some people have suffered a reduction in consumption because of taxation, while others have had their consumption boosted by an equal, compensating amount.

Net exports is the net expenditure by foreigners (which can be a negative figure) on all final goods and services produced in the economy. At this stage it can be said that national income equals $C + I + G + (X - M)$. This in turn must be further modified by *adding subsidies* and *deducting indirect taxes*. The monetary value of a loaf of bread bought by a consumer for 25p where the baker is receiving a 1p per loaf subsidy is 26p. It is from the 26p, not the 25p, that the baker pays his wages, rent, and calculates his profit. Similarly, a consumer who pays £110 for a TV set where value added tax amounts to £10 is only providing the retailer with £100 from which the retailer must pay for his productive inputs. Again, to maintain upper and lower loop identity an adjustment must be made — in the first instance by adding 1p, and in the second by deducting £10 from C.

THE INCOME APPROACH

The definition used above excluded all intermediate goods and concentrated solely on final goods and services. (Intermediate goods are those which require further processing before resale, e.g. sheet steel for car firms, flour for bakeries). Partly this exclusion is necessary to maintain the definitional identity of the two approaches to measuring national income. More importantly it is to avoid double counting and so the calculation of a higher figure for GNP than is actually the case.

Consider 2 kilograms of wheat ultimately selling for 35 pence in the form of a loaf of bread to a housewife. Assume the chain of sales and intervening processes takes place as detailed in table 2.1.

The value to the miller of 2 kilograms of wheat is 12p. That is what it is worth to him (otherwise he would not willingly part with 12p to obtain them). The miller in turn converts the grain into flour. How much effort he spends in doing so is irrelevant. What is relevant is that the baker is willing to part

Table 2.1

Transactor	Selling price	Value added
Farmer	12p	12p
Miller	20p	8p
Baker	30p	10p
Grocer	35p	5p
	97p	35p

with 20p to get the flour. The baker believes that the miller has added value of 8p to the grain. The baker converts the flour into bread and sells it to the grocer for 30p who in turn sells it to the housewife for 35p. Again, this 5p does not reflect the costs incurred by the retailer, it reflects what the housewife is willing to give up for what the retailer does (otherwise she would purchase the bread from the baker at 30p). She values the retailer's service (convenient opening hours, location, car parking facilities, the provision of convenient selling quantities, the opportunity to purchase other items simultaneously) at 5 pence. This analysis is exactly in line with our earlier discussion of marginal personal valuations and the rationale for trade and exchange. In economics value is subjective and bears little or no relation to production cost.

Value added at each stage equals selling price received at that stage less the amount paid for the intermediate product. More accurately it equals:

sales — (material + fuel purchases)

which in turn is identical to:

wages + rents + interest payments + profits (gross of corporation tax).

It is these incomes which are aggregated to obtain *gross domestic product*. If the calculation was not made in this way but rather by aggregation of selling prices then double counting would occur (e.g. in the above table a figure of 97p not 35p would be obtained). That this is erroneous can be seen by asking what would happen if the miller and baker merged. Total selling price would then equal 77 pence, yet the value of total output would remain unchanged at one loaf at 35 pence. Thus official statisticians avoid counting the same product twice in their computations. Moreover, they do so by using the value added, income aggregation approach rather than by separating the selling prices of inter-mediate and final goods. (This would be almost impossible any-way; when does a kilogram of flour represent an intermediate product for a baker and a final product for a housewife?)

To gross domestic product is added net property income from overseas, this is *gross national product*. If, as always, this does not provide the same figure for GNP as the expendi-ture approach, the latter is presumed correct and a residual adjustment made to the income approach outcome. One reason for the continual discrepancy in the two approaches is, of course, the presence of 'moonlighting' or undeclared incomes. Incomes undeclared to the Inland Revenue will not appear in the income approach yardstick, but will do so in the expenditure figures. From GNP is deducted depreciation (i.e. what firms set aside each year against profits to replace assets which are wearing out). The resultant figure is *net national product*, the strict definition of national income. The statistical annex contains information relating to some measures of British national income data for a past period of years.

PROBLEMS WITH GNP

Does GNP as a figure tell us how well off we are? Unfortu-nately there are several defects with it.

First, and obviously, countries with larger populations tend to have larger GNPs. Thus a more relevant yardstick would be GNP per capita. But per capita GNP is itself just a statistical average. It tells nothing about how the income is distributed, and if it did that would provide no further information about 'well-being'. A more equal distribution of income, it could be argued, will make people happier. It could equally easily be argued that it will do no such thing. Indeed, this point could be elaborated on and the position taken that if an equal distribution of income was imposed then the producers of GNP would be demotivated and become less productive. To the extent that producers have to share their output with non-producers then the incentive to produce will be less and both total and per capita GNP would decline.

Second, there are incomes paid out to people we wish we did not have to pay. These incomes are included in GNP. For example, the fire service, the armed forces, street sweepers and the police. Yet every time expenditure on these services increases GNP rises, but economic well-being is not necessarily improved.

Third, many desirable and undesirable goods are not traded in the market place and because they are not bought and sold in the normal way they are not added to or subtracted from GNP as a measure of economic welfare. For example, an increase in steel output raises GNP, but if it results in a dirtier atmosphere or impure river water this is not deducted from GNP. Or again, a housekeeper's services are included in GNP, but immediately she marries her employer and he ceases to pay her a formal wage GNP falls, although the services performed in the economy are unchanged. Converse examples include much charitable work which does not, nominally, raise GNP. Similarly, moves towards or away from do-it-yourself also affect GNP. Thus, a 1920's farmer who built his own barn would not have his efforts recorded in GNP, yet a farmer in 1980 who contracted the work out to a professional builder would find his expenditure included in GNP.

NOMINAL AND REAL GNP

Another problem is the distinction between nominal and real GNP. If GNP in 1970 was £200 million and by 1978 it had risen to £300 million, did economic well-being rise by 50% in that period? The answer is only 'yes' if the purchasing power of the pound had remained constant over that period. General observation tells us that the amount of goods and services a pound would buy in 1970 (its purchasing power) is not the same as it would buy in 1978. Because of a rise in average price level the value of the pound has fallen and the 50% GNP growth was merely nominal; only a part was real.

The nominal growth rate of GNP is computed by using pounds of current purchasing power, i.e. using pounds of the year for which the computation was made. In contrast, real GNP is computed using pounds of a constant or fixed purchasing power.

This is accomplished by deflating the nominal GNP by some index or group of indices to arrive at the real figure. The real figure is expressed in fixed purchasing power pounds relating to some arbitrarily chosen base year. If the objective is to examine rates of change in GNP, the choice of base year is of little relevance. There are problems with the use of indices, however.

There are two official indices, one monthly, one annual, which measure changes in consumer prices. Either of them, or a combination of the two, can be used to measure purchasing power.

The General Index of Retail Prices (RPI) is published monthly by the Department of Employment. It measures changes in the prices of a large and representative selection of goods and services. The number of separate commodities and services for which prices are regularly collected is nearly 300, and about 150,000 separate price quotations from a range of retailers throughout the country are used each month in compiling the index. The items are selected and the index is weighted in accordance with the pattern of consumption of an average family; and the weighting (the importance given to each type of spending, such as food or transport) is brought up to date each year. The 'average family' excludes households where income is either very high or where the main income is from old-age pensions or supplementary benefit. With its monthly check on prices, this index gives an up-to-date 'running commentary' on the way retail prices are moving.

The other index used in measuring the purchasing power of the pound is the Consumer Price Index (CPI), which is compiled by the Central Statistical Office and measures annual changes. It arises from the calculations used to put GNP figures on to a 'constant price' basis. In addition a further six indices are used to deflate GNP to real terms.

The reason is that the prices of different types of expenditure tend to rise at different rates, so seven principal different price indices are derived — for consumers' expenditure, exports, imports, spending on fixed assets such as buildings, roads and machinery, government and local authorities' current spending, total home spending and total spending. Consumers' spending makes up over two-thirds of the total. The RPI and the CPI differ in their coverage in the method of revaluing spending on particular goods and in the formulae used to calculate the final indices. The two indices are not entirely unconnected as roughly one quarter of the components in the RPI are reckoned up in total consumers' expenditure and the two indices tend to agree fairly closely.

Index number problems can best be explained by example. Say the Department of Employment has identified the 'typical' family's 'market basket' of the 300 most commonly purchased items for a given base year. After sampling stores it then knows, for that base year, the typical items bought by the typical family, the average quantities bought of each item and the average price for each item in the basket: all for the base year.

Table 2.2 shows how such an index would be calculated for a hypothetical four-item basket in the base year 1968. The price index is 100 for the base year, obtained by dividing total expenditure in 1968 by total expenditure in that year multiplied by 100/1, thus:

$$\text{Price index } 1968 = \frac{59}{59} \times \frac{100}{1} = 100$$

The money prices of the four items change in the decade to 1978 by the amounts shown in the table. Total expenditure rises in current pounds to £85.50. Money expenditure, how-

Table 2.2

Product	(Current £'s) 1968 price	1968 quantity	(Current £'s) 1968 expenditure	(Current £'s) 1978 price	(Current £'s) '1978 expenditure'	(1968 £'s) 1978 price	Real relative price change
Shirts	5.00	5	25.00	4.00	20.00	2.76	− 45%
Beef	0.70	10	7.00	1.20	12.00	0.83	+ 19%
Petrol	0.30	40	12.00	0.65	26.00	0.45	+ 50%
Records	3.00	5	15.00	5.50	27.50	3.79	+ 26%
			59.00		85.50		

Table 2.3 Real purchasing power of the pound (pence) (CPI, varying base years)

£1 =	1963	1964	1965	1966	1967	1968	1969	1970	1971
100p in 1963	100	97	92½	89	87	83	79	75	69½
100p in 1964	103½	100	95½	92	90	86	81½	77½	71½
100p in 1965	108	104½	100	96½	94	90	85	81	75
100p in 1966	112	108½	104	100	97½	93½	88½	84	78
100p in 1967	115	111½	106½	102½	100	95½	91	86	80
100p in 1968	120	116½	111½	107	104½	100	95	90	83½
100p in 1969	126½	122½	117½	113	110	105½	100	95	88
100p in 1970	133½	129	123½	119	116	111	105½	100	92½
100p in 1971	144	139½	133½	128½	125	120	113½	108	100

ever, has risen only by that figure deflated by the base year expenditure less 100, namely 45%. The 1978 price index is calculated thus:

$$\text{Price index } 1978 = \frac{85.50}{59.00} \times \frac{100}{1} = 145$$

And real expenditure is unchanged.

In other words, to buy the same market basket in 1978 costs £85.50. On average, prices have risen by 45%. Or, to turn it round, the 1978 £1 is only worth 69 pence of 1968 money, viz. (59.00/85.50) × 100 = 69. This is, in essence, how GNP is deflated. Table 2.3 shows the real purchasing power of the pound over a series of years.

There remain difficulties with the CPI and the other six indices used to deflate GNP in practice. These difficulties are due to changes in the 'market basket' itself. It does not remain static, and attempts to up-date the base year basket are never wholly successful and can be positively distorting.

First, products are continuously improving in quality. Refrigerators have become self-defrosting, 1978 cars are better than 1968 cars and so on. How much of the average 45% increase in price is simply due to a quality change? Second, new products appear — mini-calculators, music centres, TV games were not in the 1968 'basket' yet are bought in large numbers now. Even if the 'basket' is modified to include them, is it possible to truly compare like with like, automatic washing machines with scrubbing boards in terms of one yardstick, a constant purchasing power pound? Third, and conversely, old products disappear — cross-ply tyres, scrubbing boards and household starch are no longer bought in the same quantities as they were. Fourth, consumer tastes change — the mini-skirt, the hula-hoop, the skate-board, nylon stockings may appear in the 'basket' one year and not the next.

Not only did the 'typical' family spend its income differently in 1978 from the way it did in 1968 for these reasons, but, and less obviously, relative price changes in themselves induce a reallocation of consumer expenditures. As prices rise or fall (relative to other prices) people buy less or more of the good in question. This is a major implication of the demand curve. In table 2.2, the 1968 and 1978 current prices are shown for each of shirts, beef, petrol and records. However, if each of these prices for 1978 is deflated by the price index (divided by 145 and multiplied by 100) the 1978 price is obtained in constant purchasing power pounds. In constant pounds shirts fell in price to £2.76, a drop of 45%, beef rose to £1.20 in 1978 pounds, £0.83 in 1968 pounds, a rise of 19%, and so on. These price changes would, in themselves, alter the mix in the market basket. More shirts would be bought, and less beef and petrol and fewer records.

Thus, even ignoring the first four criticisms of index numbers, a price index will tend to give too much weight to items whose prices have risen, and too little to those whose prices have fallen. It will be too readily assumed that items which have gone up in (real) price will form the same proportion of the 'market basket' as before and vice versa. This will not be true.

However, index number deflators, for all their faults, are probably the best methods available of transforming nominal to 'real' GNP.

3
Say's Equality

Jean Baptiste Say was a nineteenth century French economist who argued that we need never fear glut since 'supply creates its own demand'. This flip slogan, which Say, in fact, never used was for long attributed to him. He was writing at a time when others such as Malthus feared overpopulation and so the slogan attributed to him had a certain appeal.

Events proved Malthus wrong, largely due to improving agricultural productivity in the Old World and the opening up of new territories in the New World. This in turn seemed to reinforce the validity of the slogan.

THE REAL MEANING OF SAY'S PRINCIPLE

Here we have a clue as to what Say really meant. He was not asserting that supply will create its own demand for the same thing. An increased supply of labour, for example, need not induce a corresponding increased demand for labour. Rather an increased supply of labour might induce, for example, an increased demand for food. Nevertheless, it was the slogan quoted above which took hold, not only of the public's mind but that of a great many economists as well.

The Depression of the 1930s seemed to nullify Say's equality. Certainly the flip slogan was negated. The supply of labour was there, why was there no demand for it?

SAY'S EQUALITY EXPLAINED[1]

Suppose all transactors are neither thieves nor philanthropists, that is all trades are voluntary on both sides. Then anyone who plans to acquire more of something must also plan to give up something in exchange. Moreover, the market values of the two commodities must be identical (since he is neither thief nor philanthropist). His source of funds for purchasing is the market price of what he plans to give up multiplied by its quantity (for example, one hour of labour times the hourly wage rate). A source of funds is obviously essential unless the economy is in a barter state.

For any individual then, his planned uses of funds must exactly offset his planned sources of funds. So for any one individual the following equation of intentions holds:

$$p_1 \, \Delta q_1 + p_2 \, \Delta q_2 + p_3 \, \Delta q_3 + \ldots + p_i \, \Delta q_i + \Delta q_m = 0$$

where there are i goods in the economy, each with a relevant price, p. In any given period an individual either plans to keep his stock of goods unchanged or plans to increase or decrease his stocks of all or some goods. If Δq is positive he has a planned excess demand, if negative a planned negative excess demand, or, what is the same thing, a planned excess supply. In addition to the i goods there is the further commodity, m, or money with a price of unity. Δq_m can also be positive, negative or zero. Finally, since he is neither thief nor philanthropist, the positive Δqs times their respective ps must equal the negative Δqs times their ps. Sources of funds must equal uses of funds. So if there is as much as one planned excess demand there must be a corresponding planned excess supply to enable the equation to sum to zero. The goods can range from cars to labour to TV sets or to bonds (i.e. the borrowing or lending of money by the sale or purchase of IOUs or certificates of indebtedness).

Now suppose there are K transactors in the economy then

---

1. This section draws on C. W. Baird, *Elements of Macroeconomics*, West 1977.

Table 3.1

	Good 1		Good 2			Good i		Money	Sum
Transactor 1	$p_1 \, \Delta q_{1,1}$	$+$	$p_2 \, \Delta q_{2,1}$	$\ldots +$		$p_i \, \Delta q_{i,1}$	$+$	$\Delta q_{m,1}$	$= 0$
Transactor 2	$p_1 \, \Delta q_{1,2}$	$+$	$p_2 \, \Delta q_{2,2}$	$\ldots +$		$p_i \, \Delta q_{i,2}$	$+$	$\Delta q_{m,2}$	$= 0$
. . . ...	. . .		. . .	...		. . .		. . .	...
. . . ...	. . .		. . .	...		. . .		. . .	...
. . . ...	. . .		. . .	...		. . .		. . .	...
Transactor K	$p_1 \, \Delta q_{1,K}$	$+$	$p_2 \, \Delta q_{2,K}$	$\ldots +$		$p_i \, \Delta q_{i,K}$	$+$	$\Delta q_{m,K}$	$= 0$
Planned market excess demands	$P_1 Q_1$		$+ \; P_2 Q_2$	$+ \; \ldots +$		$P_i Q_i$	$+$	Q_m	$= 0$

a similar equation could be set up for each as in table 3.1. Since the sum of each row is zero, the sum of the final column is zero — that is Say's principle. The sum of all planned market excess demands, over all goods, including money, is zero. It is not the flip slogan 'supply creates its own demand'. For that to be true each column would add to zero. But if we add transactor 1's planned excess demand for good 1 to transactor 2's down to transactor K's a figure of $P_1 Q_1$ will be arrived at. $P_1 Q_1$ could be positive, negative or zero, as could $P_2 Q_2$ and so on. No single market's planned excess demand need necessarily sum to zero.

GENERAL EQUILIBRIUM

Say's equality holds no matter what the price. The table must sum to zero irrespective of the levels of P_1 to P_i. In the special case where each and every market is in equilibrium (as in the market in figure 1.7) then no planned excess demand exists anywhere. This, however, only holds for one particular series of prices and is the special case known as general equilibrium (GE). Say's equality holds in GE, but it holds at all other price combinations as well. In GE the prices ruling are such that each column sums to zero. When GE does not hold, Say's principle states that if one market has a price above the GE level, then planned negative excess demand in that market exists. In which case, in at least one other market, the price must be below the GE level for there to be a compensating planned excess demand.

Table 3.2	Labour	Commodities	Bonds	Money	Total
Stage 1	0	0	0	0	0
Stage 2	0	E_S	0	E_D	0
Stage 3	E_S	0	0	E_D	0
Stage 4A	E_S	E_D	0	0	0
Stage 4B	E_S	0	0	0	<0
Stage 4C	E_S	0	0	(E_D)	(0)
Stage 4D	E_S	(E_D)	0	0	(0)

Based on (1) C.W. Baird, *Elements of Macroeconomics*, West 1977 and (2) Axel Leijonhufvud, *Keynes and the Classics*, Institute of Economic Affairs 1969.

In the ordinary case of figure 1.7 the price of the good in the market for which there is a planned excess supply would fall, and that of the good for which there is a planned excess demand would rise. GE would be restored and all plans would again be carried out. Economies do not always return to GE, however.

EFFECTIVE DEMAND FAILURE

Plans are not always carried out even when they exist, and Say's equality applies only to planned activities. Table 3.2 highlights the difference between planned and effective demands. The four markets dealt with in macroeconomics are detailed there.

Stage 1 represents general equilibrium. Total planned excess demand (E_D) in each market is zero. Stage 2 occurs if for some reason the money supply is cut[2] and households find that the average amount of money they hold is less than they would wish or plan to. They respond by curtailing expenditures on commodities in an attempt to build up their money balances. Firms, consequently, sell less than they plan to.

----

2. Either deliberately in the domestic economy (see Chapter 7) or by maintaining an artificially high foreign exchange rate (see Chapter 11), resulting in a surplus of money in the foreign exchange market and a corresponding reduction domestically.

Stage 3 occurs as firms react to the fact that unsold stocks of commodities are accumulating and so lay off labour in order to carry out their plans to sell what they actually produce. Stage 4A is arrived at when the price of commodities falls as firms eventually adjust their prices towards the level implied by the fall in demand in the move from stages 1 to 2. (Prices, as we shall learn, are rarely the first economic variables to change. Information is not free and it takes much time and effort before firms determine the optimal response to changing supply and demand conditions.) The system could move from 4A back to stage 1 by a bidding down of wages and a bidding up of commodity prices until the price vector is found where all activities and plans are perfectly coordinated.

In a monetary economy this does not happen in major depressions. The economy has moved out of what Leijonhufvud called 'the corridor' where the normal readjustment process would occur. There is no upward pressure on commodity prices. The offer of labour services (by the unemployed) does not constitute *effective* demand. Stage 4B shows how efffective demands can sum to less than zero. Stage 4C and 4D, however, illustrate how Say's principle is still not violated. The sum of *planned* demands is zero. Workers offer their labour services but, since they are not philanthropists, they *plan* to exchange these services for money (4C) or (indirectly) for money and so for goods (4D). The letters in parentheses indicate planned demands which cannot be put into effect.

According to Leijonhufvud (Baird, p. 59) this was Keynes' great contribution — namely, the identification of the problem of *effective demand failure*. Moreover, it *could only happen in a monetary economy*, not a barter economy. Workers say to employers, 'We will buy your commodities, but first you must employ us and provide us with the money to make the purchases'. Employers say to workers, 'We will take you on but first you must buy our products in order to provide us with the monetary wherewithal to pay you'. In a barter economy, the problem of the monetary linkage would not be present.

In short, Say's principle is not violated in Stage 4B which

refers to effective, not planned, supply and demand. Stage 4B refers only to offers of trade actually made. No offers to buy commodities are made although offers to sell labour (unemployment queues) are present. The plans to buy commodities are present, however, in Stage 4A. But these plans can only be carried out if the money is available. In 4C or 4D the plans cannot be put into effect for just this reason: shortage of money.

So Keynes emphasised the validity of Say's equality that the sum of planned excess demands equals zero. But he also showed how the sum of effective demands can be negative, thus negating the slogan that 'supply creates its own demand'. Effective demands can sum to less than zero because of the uniqueness of money which enters into every transaction, and because of the inflexibility of prices relative to quantity changes.

These truths, which are very simple, will be emphasised again and again in later pages. In fact ' there is hardly a single problem in macro-theory ... that can be consistently analysed without' Say's principle (Leijonhufvud, cited in Baird, p. 61).

To cite Keynes (*General Theory,* p. 235) 'unemployment develops ... because people want the moon: a man cannot be employed when *the object of desire* (i.e. money) is something which cannot be produced ... ' (emphasis added). And, of course, this all implies that if money is at the root of any economic problem the cure must lie in somehow placing money or credit in the hands of producers, who will then hire unemployed resources. This is at odds with the thinking of many of Keynes' disciples who argue that fiscal policy (cutting taxes, increasing government expenditure to place money in the hands of consumers) is the appropriate remedy for depression. The alleged manipulation of demand in this way simply results in inflation: too much money chasing too few goods. Any businessman knows that wages are paid *before* goods produced are sold and not after. For this reason *firms,* not consumers, must have money or credit before they can increase production, and they must have access to it before consumers if inflation is to be avoided. This theme will be developed in later pages.

4

The Labour Market

The labour market is one of the most emotive of the four macro-markets. Unemployment rates or percentages are frequently stated by politicians. Total absolute numbers of unemployed are also frequently bandied about in the media and in parliament. The fact that the macro-markets are aggregate markets needs to be especially carefully interpreted here. Such totals tend to ignore people as individuals. They may also obscure the underlying economics of the macro-market itself.

First, if we exclude the lame, the halt and the blind, who are the unemployed? They include new entrants to the market such as school leavers; re-entrants such as wives going back to work, unable at first to find a suitable job; those who have left their job voluntarily; and those who have been sacked.

THE DURATION OF UNEMPLOYMENT

For most people, unemployment only lasts for a short period of time while they search for work. They go on to the register of unemployed at their local labour exchange or Job Centre and out again rapidly. Table 4.1 illustrates this phenomenon. Concern should certainly be expressed for the very small percentage of total unemployed who remain searching for

Table 4.1 Expected duration of unemployment per 100 people registering as unemployed (UK).

1961–65	1967–70	Would remain after weeks
73	78	1
54	52	2
32	40	4
20	25	8
5	7	26
2	3	52

Source: John B. Wood, *How Little Unemployment?* Institute of Economic Affairs 1975; p. 16.

work after 6–12 months. The majority of people who are unemployed, however, find work after periods of over 2–4 weeks. Of course, the longer individuals take to seek for and accept a new job, the longer they remain in the total number of unemployed. The longer they search, the bigger, therefore, becomes that unemployment figure.

NATURAL UNEMPLOYMENT

Unemployment can never be zero in a complex economy. People leave school, wives go back to work, individuals change their job preferences and consumers decide to buy more of one product and less of another, thus increasing demand for workers in the former industry and decreasing it in the latter. While people are looking for a job for these reasons, unemployment exists.

Always and everywhere consumer tastes are changing. They want more of this (*A*) and less of that (*B*). If consumers should get what they want then the demand curve for good *A* will move out to the right and that for *B* in and to the left. In a market economy this is how the sovereign consumer indicates that more resources of labour and capital should be devoted to the production of *A* and less to *B*.

In a command economy planners would simply instruct some managers to close down sections of their factories and others to open up new ones. Some workers would be told to pack their bags and shift their homes and (presumably) their families. This reallocation takes time. First, the central planner must perceive the change in consumer wants. Second, he has to order the resource allocation. Third, the labour movement and factory reconstruction must take place. The first step is the critical one and the most difficult one. If it is not taken the reallocation does not take place and consumers remain dissatisfied with queues forming for A and gluts appearing of B.

In a decentralised market economy the reallocation also takes time but probably less time. The information about changing consumer tastes does not all have to be gathered and collated in a central place and perceived by a single mind. Only the several individual producers of A and B must perceive the demand shifts and since they are involved in the market places they will be the first to notice such shifts anyway. Moreover, their desire to run profitable enterprises will encourage them not only to perceive the demand shifts but to act on these shifts.

JOB SEARCH

Consider the actual working of the market, making the following most favourable assumptions:

1. People spend more on A and less on B.
2. Total spending is unchanged.
3. There is no mismatch of skills or training; those people who produce A can equally well produce B.
4. The number of jobs lost in industry B exactly equals those gained in industry A.

The original demand curves for labour (figure 4.1) are D_A and D_B (i.e. the functions showing how many workers each industry will employ at any given wage). The wage rate is W_1 in both, otherwise workers would shift from one industry to the other higher-paying industry. The original employment levels are E_A and E_B. Given assumption 1, the labour demand

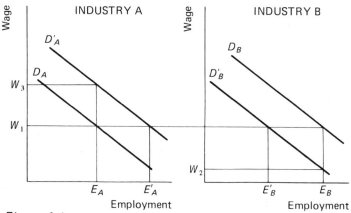

Figure 4.1

curves shift accordingly to D'_A and D'_B. In industry A either
wage levels will rise to W_3 to maintain employment, or they
will remain at W_1, increasing employment to E'_A. In industry
B wage levels will either fall to W_2 to maintain employment
or remain at W_1 reducing employment to E'_B.

If we ignore minimum wage legislation or trade union
contracts, the outcome will be the E'_A, E'_B alternative rather
than the E_A, E_B possibility. In short, some workers will
probably prefer to accept the sack rather than accept the
wage cut. The worker, in coming to that decision, will bear in
mind his value in alternative employments. The wage he is
getting now, W_1, could also be got elsewhere, and that sets
the floor to what he will accept to remain in industry B.

There is no reason for him to believe he cannot get another
job at a rate of W_1 in another industry, so, perfectly rationally,
he leaves industry B. (His search for that other job will be
more effective if he is not spending time working.) Employers
in A, meanwhile, are looking for labour. They will not hire
the first applicants, but interview, sample and test to ensure
that they are getting capable recruits. Employers will spend
time obtaining information about potential employees.

Employees, similarly, search for good jobs and do not
necessarily accept the first opening offered. When a worker
turns down a job he incurs two costs: an opportunity cost,
namely the earnings he is turning down, and a direct cost,

namely the price of the shoe leather, petrol and other expenditures he is incurring in his search. Each day he must
decide whether or not to continue searching. He will only
continue searching if the marginal benefits of search exceed
the marginal costs.

The marginal benefits are based on the *expected* difference
between the best offer received to date and the new wage
offer that he hopes may be received tomorrow (i.e. some
absolute figure multiplied by a probability factor of less than
unity). The longer he searches the more pessimistic he
becomes about discovering better wage offers and, in turn,
the lower will be the probability he will attach to finding a
better offer than the one made to date.

The marginal costs of search, on the other hand, are based
on the *actual* offers turned down, together with the actual
direct costs of an extra day's search. Diagrammatically (figure
4.2) marginal benefits (*MB*) will slope down as pessimism
increases over time. The marginal cost curve is likely to slope
up from some low point. For example, on day one, the best
offer turned down was the wage cut, W_2, itself.

For the average searcher t^* is the optimal time to spend in
job search. Less than t^* spent means that the costs of one
more day's search are less than the benefits to be gained;
greater than t^* the reverse holds. The point t^* is unknown

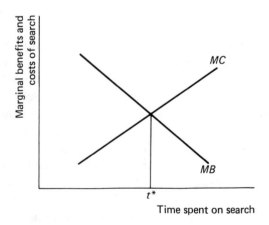

Figure 4.2

but will be greater than zero. It is greater than zero because people behave rationally and accept redundancy rather than lower wages in the hope that they will end up little or no worse off. As Keynes pointed out, wages (and other prices in other markets) are sticky downwards. This price 'stickiness' will be examined in more detail below.

Since people are always shifting their spending patterns, there will always be people in the revolving pool of unemployed. This is so even given the favourable assumptions made at the beginning of this section. The result is natural or frictional unemployment.

THE PHILLIPS CURVE AND EXPECTATIONS

Job search theory aids understanding of other phenomena. For example, if unemployment benefits rise the costs of unemployment fall. (In figure 4.2 *MC* moves to the right and so, correspondingly, does t^*.) In consequence observed unemployment rises.

In addition, one of the most puzzling economic relationships, the Phillips Curve, can also be explained. For example, suppose people have false expectations regarding the rate of inflation (i.e. the rate of increase of the general money price level). Say job searchers expect a zero rate when in actuality it is 5%. Money wage offers consequently *look* attractive. Their poor purchasing power is not appreciated. Searchers believe that they have uncovered good job opportunities quickly, they therefore believe they will be incurring a higher cost if they turn down these *apparently* attractive offers. (In figure 4.2 *MC* moves up and to the left and so, correspondingly, does t^*.) In consequence unemployment falls.

Eventually people realise they are being fooled into cutting their job search time, the wage offers they have been accepting are not that wonderful (in real terms) and *MC* shifts back to the right as people willingly forgo the apparently high, but actually poor, wage offers. Thus unexpected or unanticipated inflation can reduce unemployment but the effect is temporary (unless, of course, the inflation rate is continually increased *ahead* of peoples' expectations, something which did occur in Britain in the 1950s and 1960s).

The converse also applies. If people overestimate the inflation rate, the costs of turning down job offers are *apparently* less, *MC* moves to the right and unemployment rises. This will persist until people realise they are turning down apparently poor job offers, which in real terms are good ones.

Much of this underlies the understanding of the Phillips Curve. Phillips discovered an inverse relationship from 1861–1957 for the UK similar to that in figure 4.3. Thus governments apparently had a very useful trade-off policy tool. Whichever goal was electorally more attractive (say lower unemployment) the government simply had to raise the inflation rate. (How this can be done will be discussed later.)

The Phillips Curve has become somewhat discredited, however. First, its theoretical underpinnings have been attacked. Second, it has failed to hold true empirically elsewhere or at other times. Third, as noted above, to reduce unemployment permanently, according to search theory, requires an ever-increasing rate of inflation.

The theory of the Phillips Curve is persuasively simple and is outlined in figure 4.4. At *e* the labour market is in equilibrium at wage rate W_e and employment level E. Unemployment is zero (or at the 'natural' or 'frictional' rate). At W_f there is a shortage of labour and an upward pressure on wage

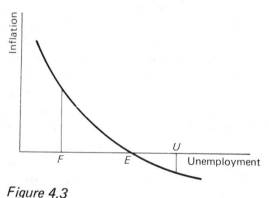

Figure 4.3

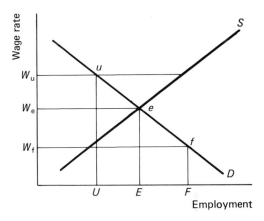

Figure 4.4

rates (unemployment is low, wages are rising, a situation like
F in figure 4.3). At W_u, there is a surplus of labour and a
downward pressure on wage rates (unemployment is high,
and inflation is low, analogous to point *U* in figure 4.3). To
quote Friedman, 'the fallacy in Phillips is that once you
(explicitly) label the vertical axis *W/P* (where *P* is the average
of all other prices, so that 'wage rate' is the 'real' not the
money wage rate) the graph has nothing to say about what is
going to happen to *nominal wages* or prices'.[1] In fact if
either W or *P* rise or fall, provided they both do so, and do
so at the same rate, then employment levels and *real* wages
will be constant.

Phillips, of course, was not being quite so disingenuous as to
ignore the fact that the vertical axis of supply and demand
diagrams is always implicitly, although seldom explicitly,
calibrated in real terms. Given that Keynes pointed out that
prices are sticky, Phillips was merely simplifying his argument
to say that changes in *anticipated nominal* wages were the
same thing as changes in *anticipated real* wages. But in the
presence of *unanticipated* inflation this house of cards
collapses. In the event of inflation, actual *real* wages can be
very different from anticipated real wages.

---

1. Milton Friedman, *Unemployed versus Inflation?* Institute of Economic Affairs 1975, p. 15.

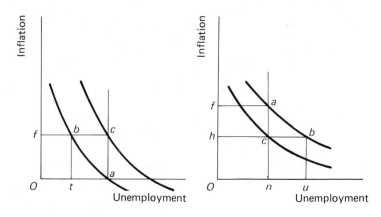

(a) Effect of increased inflation rate   (b) Effect of decreased inflation rate

Figure 4.5

This was shown in the discussion surrounding figure 4.2 and can now easily be transferred to the Phillips framework as in figure 4.5.

In figure 4.5(a) the natural unemployment level is at a point *a*. Inflation is zero. Assume the inflation rate is now increased to *f*. This induces job searchers to accept offers quickly and cut their search time while continuing to expect zero inflation. Unemployment falls to *t* and the economy moves up the Phillips curve from *a* to *b*. Job seekers eventually realise that the 'attractive' job offers they are receiving are not as good as they anticipated in real terms. They increase their search period. The economy moves from *b* to *c*. Unemployment returns to *a*, its natural level, and the Phillips curve can either be regarded as redundant or as having shifted to the right. There is no long-run trade-off between inflation and unemployment (unless inflation is persistently increased) and the long-run Phillips curve is essentially a vertical line passing through *a*.

Conversely, in figure 4.5(b), at *a* the inflation rate is *f*, but unemployment is at its natural level. If government now attempts to cut the inflation rate, the initial impact is for unemployment to move to *u*, the economy moves to *b*, and inflation is *h*. People receive lower money wage offers and so wait longer before accepting employment. Time is required

before they realise that the inflation rate has in fact fallen
and that they are turning down wages which in real purchasing
power terms are high. When they adjust their anticipations to
the new, lower inflation rate they will reduce their job search
time, u will fall to n, and the economy move back to c.
Again, the long-term Phillips curve seems to be a vertical line.

From a policy viewpoint the questions are: (1) Is ever-
increasing inflation desirable to keep unemployment below
its natural level? and (2) Given inflation, how long a period
will have to elapse before the community adjusts its inflationary anticipations and so reduces its job search period to
levels permitting natural unemployment to be attained? In
the 1950s and 1960s and early 1970s in Britain the answer to
question (1) appeared to be positive (in the eyes of the
politicians). The second question has had an answer of 18—24
months provided by some authorities, with longer periods for
higher inflation rates. If this period of above-natural unemployment stretches out towards an election campaign politicians
may well opt again for the ever-increasing inflationary route.

STRUCTURAL UNEMPLOYMENT

Here the favourable assumption that workers who are suited
to industry A are also suited to industry B is abandoned. In
short, there is a mismatch between the skills and training
demanded by the expanding industry and those made redundant in the declining industry. Locations may also differ.
Those laid off in B will, as before, refuse a wage cut to stay
employed, but their job search will be unsuccessful. Normally,
it would be expected that as soon as they realised this they
would move to a job in A for a lower wage during a period
of on-job training (until their skills were worth the going
wage in industry A) but trade unions in industry A or minimum wage legislation will prevent employers offering a
sufficiently low wage to attract such workers. Another
obstacle might be location. If local authorities where A is
sited do not permit incoming workers access to council
houses but make them join existing queues based on residence

periods in the locality, then the workers will be forced to stay in their existing houses in that part of the country where B is situated.

They will join the ranks of the hard core unemployed; those with obsolete skills, no training, no education or the disabled. Of course, this need not be the case. In the absence of central or local government laws and rules, in the absence of trade unions, they could have obtained work, and their wage would have risen as their productivity increased. (If it had not done so automatically then competition between employers in industry A, as each made bids for the skilled men, would have ensured that incomes did rise.)

DECLINING AGGREGATE DEMAND AND PRICE 'STICKINESS'

The assumption that although demand for B falls it is compensated for (in employment terms) by a rise in demand for goods produced by industry A is now dropped. Aggregate GNP falls. This could mean either of two things. Initially the following situation exists.

$$Y_1 = P_1 Q_f$$
where $Y_1 = \text{GNP}$
P_1 = the average price level
Q_f = the volume of goods produced at full employment given natural unemployment.

If GNP now falls to Y_2 this could imply either that

$$Y_2 = P_2 Q_f \ldots (1)$$
or that
$$Y_2 = P_1 Q_2 \ldots (2)$$

The fall in total spending (by households, firms or government) is the result either of falling average prices (to P_2) so that real GNP and employment are unchanged (equation 1) or it takes the form of steady prices, falling real GNP and lower output and employment (to Q_2 in equation 2).

Whether prices or real GNP fall first is obviously critical.

Keynes suggested that prices will not be the first economic variables to change. Prices react more slowly than quantities, therefore unemployment will rise in the face of a decline in total expenditure.

Information is not free. Any seller of anything (commodities, labour or bonds) is interested in his average rate of sale, but each seller experiences occasions when sales are exceptionally high or low (e.g. pre-Christmas in toy stores, dead of winter in ice-cream shops). A demand curve, therefore, does not show specific sales rates at different prices, but only *average* sales rates. Around each point on a demand curve there is, at the given price, a *distribution* of quantities, but the curve itself shows only the mean. That, of course, is why businessmen carry stocks. They are used as buffers which permit *transitory* changes in sales rates away from the normal run of business.

When aggregate demand falls many sellers (not necessarily all) find their demand curves have shifted leftwards. Each individual seller involved knows his sales have fallen. But he can interpret this fall in two ways: either it is a transient and temporary downswing peculiar to himself or to one given day or period, or it is due to a reduction in aggregate spending in the economy. If he interprets it as a normal short-term trading downturn he will expect sales to pick up soon. In that case he will not lower his price.

It takes a relatively prolonged period before individual sellers realise that demand has definitely and permanently shifted leftwards and downwards. When this is realised a new, lower price is required to maintain the original *average* sales rate. The period taken to realise that demand has fallen is lengthened by the fact that even the *new* average will have transient upswings and downswings in sales rates around it. This in turn could further mislead the seller into thinking the old average has not shifted. There is a lot of noise in the system.

The labour market is no different from the commodity market. Redundant workers, as sellers of labour, do not immediately realise that aggregate demand has fallen. They seek for new jobs at their old wage rates, so prolonging the period of search and enlarging the pool of unemployed. They do not immediately perceive that demand for labour as a whole has fallen and so they turn down money wage offers not realising that they are the best that can be obtained in real terms.

As firms eventually calculate the best (lower) prices, and as workers gradually reduce the wage offers they will accept, prices eventually decline and, if the decline is identical, $Y_2 = P_2 Q_f$ will obtain. Real income will be unchanged. This period of adjustment to a fall in aggregate demand can take time, and during that period prices, wages and unemployment can be higher than their equilibrium levels. The original classical view is that if prices and wages fall, employment will eventually be restored. This is true if wages and prices adjust both far enough and immediately (for example, simultaneously or nearly so in Stages 2 and 3 of table 3.2 above). However, during the Depression years this did not happen. Between 1930 and 1933 money wages fell 4.3%, money prices fell 11.4%, yet unemployment rose from around 1½ million to 2½ million.

What Keynes called 'involuntary' unemployment due to 'effective demand failure' had occurred. Economies encounter this if they run out of back-up sources of money. To demand labour effectively firms require money. As Robert Clower stated: 'Money buys goods and goods buy money: but goods do not buy goods.'[2] In table 3.2, this is epitomised in Stage 4C. No demand exists for goods, no offers to sell goods are made, and no plans to buy goods are made, yet there is a negative excess demand for labour (the unemployed) and a positive planned excess demand for money, just as Say's equality suggests.

Is classical supply and demand analysis of little use? As long as the decline in aggregate demand is not too dramatic the answer is 'no'. Only if the economy is forced out of a safety zone, known by Leijonhufvud as the 'corridor', will price adjustments shortly (not immediately) restore the economy to a full employment position. If, however, any

2. Cited in C.H. Baird, *op. cit.*, p. 80.

shock the economy suffers is severe other measures may also be required. (Some, such as Keynes, recommended fiscal policy, others recommend monetary policy and still others choose wage and price controls.) Since major shocks are rare, however, it could be argued that frequent active policy measures by government are unnecessary. They will be convulsive rather than stabilising in nature. Information is not free to government any more than it is to the market participants. Government will thus receive information more belatedly than the market participants themselves. Central collection, collation and action is necessary and this, of necessity, must be slower than the diffuse action taken by dispersed market participants who perceive relevant market movements almost immediately.

5

The Keynesian Cross

National income was seen to be measured by two alternative methods: the income and the expenditure approaches. The two techniques, subject to normal statistical errors, gave identical results. This can be illustrated diagrammatically in figure 5.1. The vertical axis indicates the sum of all actual expenditures by households, firms and government on consumption, investment and government spending respectively (viz. actual $C + I + G$). The horizontal axis represents the total monetary value of all final goods and services produced in the economy and is obtained by aggregating all incomes or 'value added'.

INCOME AND ACTUAL EXPENDITURES

If the axes are drawn up on the same scale then it is merely a matter of geometric definition that the 45° line passing through the origin shows all points where the two approaches to GNP measurement (excluding foreign trade for the moment) provide the expected identical answers. To ensure that the two approaches to the measurement of GNP always provide a result which lies on the 45° line the definitions were carefully constructed (Chapter 2). Principally, if total purchases are less than what business produces then stock building by business is regarded as investment expenditure by business.

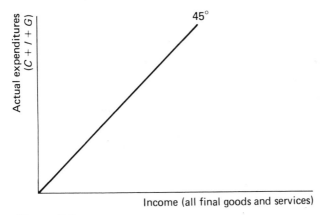

Figure 5.1

Conversely, if total purchases exceed production then stock reduction must occur and this inventory depletion is regarded as negative investment or disinvestment.

Thus *actual* total investment equals purchases of new plant, equipment, factory buildings and planned stock increases *plus* any *unplanned* stock changes. Unintended inventory changes are defined as *unplanned investment*. Only the *I* component of *C + I + G* contains this passively determined element. *C* and *G* are always assumed to be the results of purposive acts. These planned expenditures are depicted in figure 5.2.

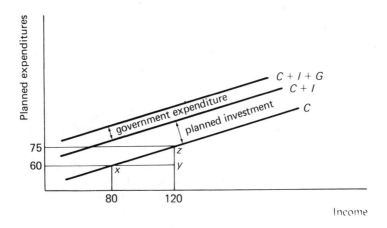

Figure 5.2

INCOME AND PLANNED EXPENDITURES

C shows what households in aggregate plan to spend at different income levels and *simultaneously* what they actually do spend. Thus at income level £80M they plan to and actually do spend £60M. I, however, merely shows what firms plan to invest at any income level, and this is the vertical distance between C and $C + I$. (For simplicity, I is assumed unchanged by income level and so $C + I$ is parallel to C.) *Planned I* can be expected to be further above C in times of low interest rates and closer to C in times of high interest rates.

The funds for investment come from either household or business savings (i.e. retained profits and depreciation charges in company accounts). Household savings will be higher in times of high interest rates. Households can then get a relatively high return from interest-bearing bank accounts or bonds. Thus if businesses wish to gain access to household savings they must attract these savings by offering still higher interest rates. This will discourage investment. Similarly, the higher the interest rate firms themselves can get for putting their money into bank accounts or government bonds, the less willing will they be to tie money up in plant and equipment.

G, government expenditure (excluding transfer payments) is also assumed to remain unchanged irrespective of income level and so $C + I + G$ is drawn parallel to $C + I$.

INCOME DETERMINATION

Figure 5.3 superimposes the previous two diagrams and in a simple fashion depicts the 'Keynesian cross' and its use in explaining the determination of equilibrium national income.

At income or GNP level of Y_2 planned spending is $Y_2 f$, actual spending is $Y_2 d$. There is df of unplanned spending, i.e. of unplanned investment. In particular, surprise stock-piling is occuring. Many (not necessarily all) firms are not selling the commodities they anticipated. These firms cut back on production which implies lower income levels and employ-

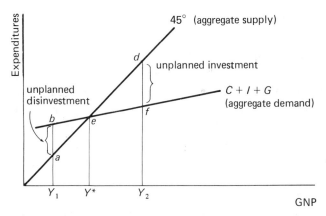

Figure 5.3

ment, so the economy moves from Y_2 leftwards to Y^*. At GNP level Y_1 total spending is Y_1b, but firms are only producing goods and services to the value of Y_1a. Incomes are being paid out of only Y_1 in terms of value added (wages and profits). Thus unplanned inventory depletion takes place. Firms increase output in response to this situation to restore stocks to their desired levels. Higher production leads to higher incomes and the economy moves from Y_1 to Y^*.

At Y^* there is no incentive for firms in the aggregate to expand or contract production. So long as aggregate transactors' plans do not change from those depicted by the aggregate demand line, GNP will remain as indicated by the equilibrium point *e*. Within that equilibrium individual firms and households would, of course, still be able to revise their individual plans (the purpose of microeconomics is to study such movement). Moreover, Y^* tells us nothing about the way its components (average price and quantity) have moved when Y_1 or Y_2 have been spontaneously abandoned as disequilibrium points. It is a presumption, and one with no theoretical foundation whatever, to imagine that prices have remained stable and only output has changed. It is equally presumptuous to claim that prices have moved, in *any* direction. To base policy prescriptions on the Keynesian cross, which takes no account of the fact that *it* makes no allowance for price movements or for their direction, is, therefore, a very risky procedure indeed.

CONSUMPTION AND SAVING FUNCTIONS

The main component of the Keynesian cross is the consumption function. It shows the relationship between aggregate consumption and aggregate income. In figure 5.2 it slopes up from left to right indicating that as GNP (more strictly, disposable income) increases so do expenditures. It is not, of course, necessary for *all* individuals to increase their expenditures as income increases. It merely implies that at an average or aggregate level they will do so.

Two concepts can now be introduced which will be referred to frequently: the average and the marginal propensities to consume. The average propensity to consume (APC) is equal to aggregate consumption expenditure divided by aggregate income. Thus at x in figure 5.2 APC = 0.75, and at z the APC = 0.625. The marginal propensity to consume (MPC) is the additional consumption expenditures induced by one extra pound of income. Thus in figure 5.2, between x and y, 40 extra units of income induce 15 extra units of consumption. The MPC is thus $15/40 = 0.375$. It is zy/xy, the slope of C. The MPC is the slope of C, and if C is a curve it will thus vary along its length.

The saving function is derived directly from C and simply shows the relationship between aggregate saving and income. Households can either spend or save their disposable incomes. Since C is expenditure on all newly produced goods and services (excluding houses) all other uses of disposable income such as purchasing bonds, increasing deposits in bank accounts, or the holding of currency are considered to be saving. (Purchases of new houses are both saving and investment.) Thus in figure 5.4(b) it is a simple matter to draw in the saving function based on the information provided in the consumption function of figure 5.4(a).

At income of 1600 where expenditure is also 1600, saving is zero. At income of 1800 where expenditure is 1700 (the gap wx) saving is 100, and correspondingly, where income is 1400, expenditure 1500 (the gap yz), dissaving is 100. Similar exercises can be carried out for other points on C and the saving function S can then be constructed as shown ($wx =$

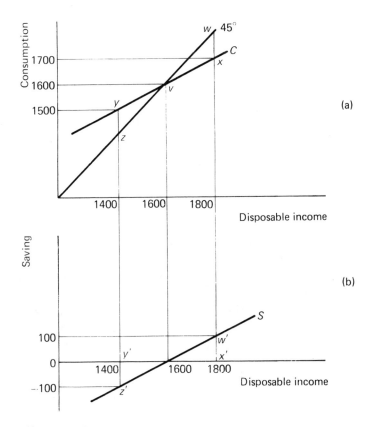

Figure 5.4

$w'x'$ and $yz = y'z'$).[1] The one function is merely the obverse of the other.

Expenditures are determined in three main ways. First, if income changes there is a movement *along* the consumption function. Second, if interest rates rise the reward from buying bonds, and so from abstaining from consumption, rises. The consumption function consequently moves down over its entire length. This is a shift *of* the consumption function. The saving function is correspondingly affected. And, conversely, if interest rates fall the reverse occurs. Finally, expec-

---

1. Note 'saving' as discussed here is a verb and should not be confused with accumulated 'savings', a noun. Each Keynesian cross diagram, like any supply and demand diagram, refers to a specific time period during which the relevant verbs are operative.

tations can induce shifts *of* the consumption function. Thus if consumers expect next year's prices to be higher than this year's they will try to buy before prices rise. They will spend more of their current income than they otherwise would. C will shift up, and S down if there are increases in the expected rate of inflation and, vice versa, spending will be deferred if prices are expected to fall.

PERMANENT INCOME[2]

Consumption functions in most texts are drawn as in figure 5.4. At v, the APC = 1, to the left and right of v the APC is greater and lesser than unity respectively. This implies that the rich spend a smaller proportion of their income than the poor. It also suggests that as a nation grows wealthier and wealthier the proportion of GNP which is consumption gets smaller and smaller and so, in order for that economy to stay at an equilibrium income level (e.g. e in figure 5.3), the proportion of GNP required of either investment or government expenditure will have to become continuously larger.

Is figure 5.4 valid and are the inferences drawn from it correct? Consumption functions in reality are constructed either on a cross-section or a time series basis. That is, in Britain, for example, for cross-sectional purposes, the government's Family Expenditure Survey could be studied for any *one* year. This classifies households by income size and provides data on their expenditure. Thus an average expenditure for the average family in a range of income groups from the lowest to the highest is obtained for that year. To this data the statistician can fit a plotted line representing the consumption function, for that year. Such studies tend to provide, for the year in question, consumption functions like C in figure 5.4 or C_{cs} in figure 5.5.

Time series data, on the other hand, do not take one point in time and analyse the community. Rather the whole popula-

---

2. Permanent income was first discussed by Milton Friedman in *The Theory of the Consumption Function*, Princeton 1958.

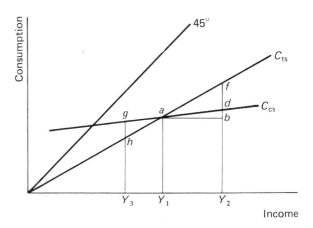

Figure 5.5

tion is examined over a run of years. It is a long-run rather than a short-run approach. Consumption data for the whole population are plotted against income for all of the years (or periods) under examination. These studies tend to provide consumption functions rather like C_{ts} in figure 5.5, which, since they pass through the origin and do not cross the $45°$ line, have the properties of constant APCs and of APC = MPC (this latter property depends on C being a straight line).

Which of the two approaches to the estimation of C is more valid? What implications does this have for the two assertions made at the beginning of this section?

Consider the reasons why people differ in their short- and long-run spending behaviour. People base their consumption plans on their expected normal, long-run average or 'permanent incomes'. They do not consume according to the level of their immediate or current incomes. A person usually has some idea what his normal income will be for the next few years at least. If he receives an unexpected windfall in his income he will not spend it to the same extent as if he thought that that income change was to be permanent. Rather he would consider himself to be lucky and save an above-average proportion of it as a cushion against transitory periods of below normal income. For example, if an individual expected the following income stream:

Year	1	2	3	4	5
Income(£)	1000	2000	10000	1000	5000

it is very unlikely that he would *consistently* spend, say, 90 per cent of the relevant income each year, particularly in year 3. Rather, an above-average proportion of year 3's income would be saved to increase consumption in year 4. Similarly, in years 1 and 2 it is very unlikely that exactly £900 and £1800 would be spent. The individual would borrow against the expected higher receipts in years 3 and 5 in order to raise consumption levels.

Permanent income theory suggests that people iron out their consumption patterns in just this way. Thus people avoid periods of feast and famine and instead enjoy a relatively steady and moderate standard of consumption over time, on a long-run or 'permanent' basis. Permanent income on this view is some sort of expected average or normal income level. Temporary or short-period income, in contrast, can exceed permanent income. When temporary income is greater than permanent income most of it will be saved and, conversely, when temporary income is less than normal income, dissaving will occur. Thus, according to permanent income theory, the true consumption function is C_{ts} and the horizontal axis should be measured in units of permanent income.

This, if correct, should make politicians exceedingly cautious in their use of National Income data. For example, in figure 5.5, if permanent income was Y_1 and in any given period actual measured or temporary income rose to Y_2 then actual measured consumption would rise only from Y_1a to Y_2d. (A rise in consumption from b to f would occur only if and when the income rise was deemed to be permanent.) Conversely, if actual income fell from a level of Y_1 to a measured level of Y_3 consumption would fall from Y_1a to Y_3g. (Consumption would only drop by a more extreme amount to Y_3h if and when, and if ever, people believed the move to Y_3 to be permanent.) Initially, in the short run, people consume out of savings: a thing they cannot do in the long run.

Thus, permanent income theory indicates that consumption

functions are much steeper than any inspection of current data would indicate. This does not support the view that the rich save more than the poor, nor does it suggest that the argument that wealthier economies must have ever larger (in relative terms) investment expenditures and government sectors is a valid one.

A WARNING

It has already been shown that there are dangers in the use of the Keynesian cross since it makes no distinction between real and money levels of GNP (GNP $= P \times Q$, and a rise in either P or Q could raise GNP on the Keynesian cross diagram). If this fact is ignored then any attempt by government to change GNP could introduce more instability into the system than otherwise (inflation might be encouraged, for example, with no corresponding real gains, but only the losses which tinkering with the price mechanism induces).

Now a further *caveat* must be given. If permanent income theory is correct then any policy actions taken as a result of short-run measured changes in consumption may exaggerate the impact of such changes. For example, if government considers it desirable for any reason to increase GNP, say, from Y_1 in figure 5.5 (because of the imminence of an election or whatever) then the short-run impact on measured consumption will be far less than the long-run impact. Yet it is the short-run change and the short-run impact which is acted upon and evaluated for purposes of *further* policy actions.

If the measured outcome is regarded as too small, then further government action may be taken. In brief a faulty interpretation of what is really happening in the economy may be made and the result will be more instability, not less. The converse is also true. If government wishes to see consumption fall to h in figure 5.5 short-run actions and measurements will provide and indicate a decline to only g. Further action may then be taken. In the long run the initial action might well have been sufficient. With further action, the short-run objective of h might well be attained but the long-run outcome might be far lower.

These effects are clearly to be deplored. But since the Keynesian cross is essentially a tool to analyse the causes of short-run rises and falls in GNP and to suggest policy prescriptions to offset such undesirable fluctuations, it is consequently difficult to avoid the pitfalls.

The main tool used in the Keynesian prescription is fiscal policy. This too can provide appealingly simple answers, but there can be dangerously misleading ones also. These are examined in the next chapter.

6
Fiscal Policy

Fiscal policy is the Keynesian prescription for managing the economy by varying the level of taxation and/or government expenditure. As we have seen, to be successful this requires (impossibly?) careful timing. Fiscal policy is geared to countering the effects of booms and slumps and to raising the general level of GNP. Before examining policy in detail a number of related or pertinent concepts must first be studied.

INVESTMENT AND SAVING

Investment, the purchase by firms of new factories or plant, the purchase by households of new houses, and the *planned* or *unplanned* net addition by firms to stocks, must be financed. Firms can acquire funds by saving (i.e. retaining profits or making depreciation provisions) or by selling shares or by borrowing. All of these sources of funds spring from saving and it is household saving which provides the funds business saving does not (either directly by the purchase of shares or loan stock or indirectly via intermediate borrowers and lenders such as banks and insurance and pension funds).

Firms must pay interest to obtain funds. ('Interest' may have different names, e.g. dividends on shares, interest on loans, 'implicit interest on or opportunity cost' of retained earnings where other returns are forgone by buying a new machine, say, instead of putting the funds in an explicit interest-bearing locale such as a bank; but 'interest' is the generic name in macroeconomics for all of these and other costs which must be incurred to obtain funds for investment.)

Interest then is the cost of investing, and it must be borne whether the funds are internally or externally generated. The higher the rate which must be paid to obtain money from households, the higher too is the opportunity cost of retained funds. (If households have good interest rate opportunities then such openings will be available to firms too. The firm forgoes such openings and their potential benefits, that is, it incurs an interest cost, if it uses retained earnings to buy new plant or equipment.) It is interest, not the price paid for a new machine or whatever, which is the cost of investing. The latter is merely a rearrangement of the firm's assets into a different form. The expense is the using up of these assets, namely the interest charge. Of course, the firm will only buy the machine in the first instance if it expects its return to be greater than its interest expense.

To households, however, interest is not a cost but a benefit. It is the reward for abstinence from consumption. It is the extra real goods and services that can be bought tomorrow when the interest payment is received. Thus if a household lends £100 and receives back £105 in a year's time the interest rate, 5%, is equal to £5 worth of goods and services which could not otherwise have been bought at the year's commencement. Similarly, the firm forgoes these goods and services when it repays the loan of £100 and the £5 of interest.

Clearly, it is real goods and services which both borrowers and lenders are concerned with. Thus if the CPI had risen 5% during the period of the example the real rate of interest would have been zero. No extra goods or services could have been bought by the lender, nor would they have been given up by the borrower. So the real rate of interest is the nominal rate of interest less the inflation rate.

Investment is therefore determined by two factors: the rate of interest and the state of expectations regarding the future revenues and costs for any given investment project.

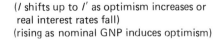

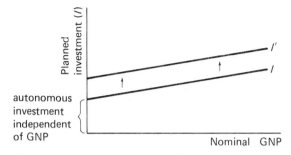

Figure 6.1

Keynes referred to the marginal efficiency of capital, a concept similar, although not totally so, to investor expectations. When the marginal efficiency of capital rises investors have become more optimistic, and vice versa. Thus for any given marginal efficiency of capital, investment will rise or fall inversely with the interest rate.

Investor optimism can be affected not only by the marginal efficiency of capital, but also by the level of GNP itself. A higher GNP may well induce a higher level of investment in addition to the already autonomous *I* existing because of current interest rates and the current marginal efficiency of capital (this argument is illustrated in figure 6.1).

If a saving schedule is superimposed on figure 6.1 (figure 6.2) it can be shown that the economy is in equilibrium (i.e.

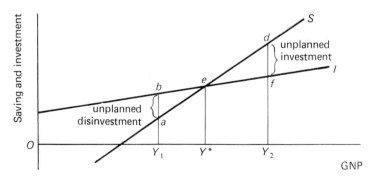

Figure 6.2

there are no surprise or unplanned stock or inventory changes) when $S = I$. The argument is similar to that employed in figure 5.3. At income or GNP level Y_2 planned investment is $Y_2 f$, while the funds coming forward for investment exceed that amount by df. Since what is saved is not spent, unplanned stockpiling is forced to take place. Firms cut back on production and the economy moves to Y^*. At Y_1 firms plan to invest $Y_1 b$ but receive insufficient funds from households (only $Y_1 a$). But since the *planned* investment is carried out and the funds to pay for it are inadequate (the unprovided funds have been used on consumption) inventory depletion must take place. Firms react by hiring more men and increasing production until GNP rises to Y^*. The economy on this view always tends towards equilibrium where S equals planned I. At any other GNP level saving also equals investment (but *not* planned investment).

THE MULTIPLIER

Consider a firm which spends £100,000 on new plant. This sum is added to the I schedule in the Keynesian cross for the period in which it is spent. But the addition to total expenditure does not cease at this point. The £100,000 goes to households, directly or indirectly, in the form of wages, salaries, dividends and so on, that is, the incomes of those who are involved in the construction of the plant (builders, shareholders, engineers, etc) are duly increased. Assume the MPC of these households is 0.9, then in addition to the £100,000 spent on I, the relevant households will spend a further £90,000 on C. But that additional £90,000 will in turn be spent on goods and services provided by firms, who in turn will pass it on as incomes to other households, who in their turn will spend it on still further goods and services (given the same MPC £90,000 × 0.9 will be spent in the next round). The cycle will continue until the figures become insignificantly small. Table 6.1 summarises the above discussion.

The initial £100,000 of I is multiplied by 10. This factor is the multiplier, and it is equal to

Table 6.1

	New expenditure (£'000)	Source
Row 1	100	original new *I*
Row 2	90	90% of original *I*
Row 3	81	90% of new *C* in row 2
Row 4	72.9	90% of new *C* in row 3
	. . .	. . .
	. . .	. . .
	. . .	. . .
Total	£1000	

$$1/(1 - \text{MPC}) = 1/0.1 = 10$$

This can be proved as follows (where *M* is the multiplier and *K* is the original addition to *I*):

$$MK = K + \text{MPC}.K + \text{MPC}^2.K + \text{MPC}^3.K$$

Therefore

$$M = 1 + \text{MPC} + \text{MPC}^2 + \text{MPC}^3 \ldots + \text{MPC}^n \qquad (1)$$

and

$$M(\text{MPC}) = \text{MPC} + \text{MPC}^2 + \text{MPC}^3 + \text{MPC}^4 \ldots + \text{MPC}^{n+1} \qquad (2)$$

Subtract equation (2) from equation (1).

$$M - M(\text{MPC}) = 1$$

Therefore

$$M (1 - \text{MPC}) = 1$$
so $\quad M = 1/(1 - \text{MPC}).$

Figure 6.3 shows the operation of the multiplier on both a Keynesian cross diagram and its *S* and *I* equivalent. *I* rises to *I'* by *x*, but the new equilibrium income level of *Y'* is $10x$ above its original level.

1. Sir John Hicks, *The Crisis in Keynesian Economics*, Basic Books, 1979, p. 27.

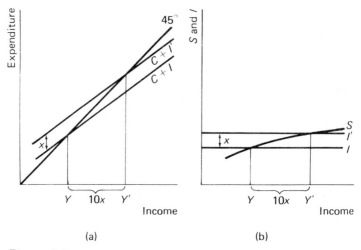

Figure 6.3

The multiplier concept must be treated with care. It only works under certain conditions. To work smoothly 'as Keynes envisaged, requires the presence of surplus stocks'.[1] Otherwise, without slack in the economy 'bottlenecks' (or inflation) will occur, as too much money chases too few goods. The movement from Y to Y' will be a money change only, not a real GNP increase.

It must not simply represent a diversion of spending from one component of the aggregate demand line $(C + I + G)$ to another (I). Otherwise the aggregate demand line will simply remain in an unchanged position. (Geometrically it is easy to see how the multiplier concept will work on any component of the $C + I + G$ line. It is not restricted to investment). It must arise either from an addition to the economy's money supply or from money withdrawn from idle hoards (or the expenditure cannot take place). The investment must be additional and new activity, otherwise the I schedule would not move at all. Finally, aggregate demand must be maintained at its new higher level if the new equilibrium is to be sustained. If it is not, the $C + I$ line will again simply fall back to its original position as soon as the new investment activity ceases.

This last point is emphasised by the associated concept of

the accelerator (which in turn may be one partial explanation of economic upswings and downswings).

THE ACCELERATOR

The demand for investment goods is derived from the demand for final goods. The fact that demand is derived helps explain the high volatility of demand in capital goods industries, as opposed to consumer goods industries. This is due to the principle of the accelerator. Table 6.2 illustrates the accelerator in action; here we have a firm which in year 1 has sales of its final product of £12M, a stock of 10 fully employed machine tools, each of differing ages, with one wearing out each year. Years 1 to 3 illustrate the firm passing through a phase of steady demand. Derived demand for machine tools is also constant, at one machine per annum, costing £6M. In year 4 final demand increases by 50% to £18M. The machine tool stock must also increase by 50% which increases the firm's purchases of machine tools from one (replacement tool) to six in total; an increase, not of 50%, but of 500%. Now, however, in years 5 and 6, final demand has got to continue growing if the derived demand for machine tools is to remain steady. This is an impossible condition. In year 7 final demand levels off at £30 million. The firm now needs no additional

Table 6.2 The acceleration principle: the relationship between demand fluctuations for consumer goods and related producers' goods

Year	Sales of final product (£M)	Stock of machine tools No. (£M)		Replacement purchases of machine tools No.	(£M)	Additional purchases of machine tools No.	(£M)	Total purchases of machine tools No.	(£M)
1	12	10	60	1	6	0	0	1	6
2	12	10	60	1	6	0	0	1	6
3	12	10	60	1	6	0	0	1	6
4	18	15	90	1	6	5	30	6	36
5	24	20	120	1	6	5	30	6	36
6	30	25	150	1	6	5	30	6	36
7	30	25	150	1	6	0	0	1	6
8	24	24	144	0	0	0	0	0	0

tools, already having the requisite 25 in hand provided one
obsolete one is replaced.

Derived demand falls from £36 million to £6 million, with
no change in final demand, only a cessation of growth. The
accelerator can also work in reverse. In year 8 final demand
falls. The firm only needs 20 machine tools. It has 25 in
stock, the one obsolete machine is not replaced reducing
stock to 24. Derived demand falls to zero, and with it falls
investment in the $C + I + G$ schedule, and a multiplied
reduction in GNP occurs.

This example is, of course, extreme. It assumes that equipment is used to the full in year 1. It assumes no technological
advance in machine tools which would stimulate their demand
with no need for a demand change in the final market. It
ignores the impact of expectations. Final producers will only
produce, or fail to replace capital equipment, if they envisage
that a demand change is likely to be fairly permanent. The
accelerator principle probably cannot be used as a mechanical
device to predict changes in derived demand or in economic
activity as a whole. However it would be foolish to ignore its
value as an indicator of possible change.

THE ALLEGED PARADOX OF THRIFT

Funds for investment come from business or household saving.
The paradox of thrift implies, however, that saving can be
injurious, that investment may be reduced and GNP lowered
as a result of increased saving. Can this paradox be explained?
Once explained, can it be resolved and shown to be fallacious?
The answer to both questions is the common sense response
'yes'. Saving is good for the economy and for investment.
Consider figure 6.4. Initially the economy is in equilibrium
at point e, investment is at level X, and GNP at Y. Now if
householders decide to save more (i.e. consume less) at each
and every income level, the saving schedule S shifts up to S'.
Equilibrium is reattained at e', GNP falls to Y' and investment
is now lower at X'. Paradoxically when households try to
save more they end up saving less. They may now be saving a

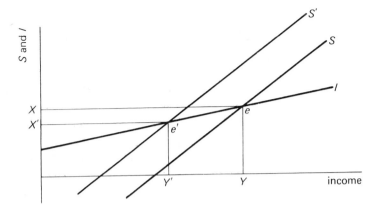

Figure 6.4

higher percentage of their new incomes, but that higher percentage is smaller in absolute terms than the figure they were saving before the shift in their desire to save more at each income level. Moreover, the decrease in consumption has been multiplied with a similar outcome to that which would have resulted from a fall in the *I* schedule; the reduction in GNP is much greater than the 'increase' in saving.

Saving is consequently a phenomenon to be condemned. It reduces GNP, reduces the level of investment, and increases unemployment. This is the natural outcome of the explanation of the paradox. To purchase tinsel is of more import than to try to make funds available for investment. After all *X'* is below *X* in investment terms.

Leijonhufvud states that this explanation is not only fallacious but is 'murderously dangerous nonsense'.[2] Table 6.3,

Table 6.3

	Labour market	Consumer goods market	Capital goods market	Bond market	Money market
1. General equilibrium	0	0	0	0	0
2. After upward shift of saving schedule	0	ES	?	?	?

2. Cited in Baird, *op. cit.*, p. 109.

based on Say's equality, explains why. Stage 1 is general equilibrium, where supply and demand in each of the five markets in the economy are equal. In addition, in accordance with Say's equality, the sum of the planned excess demands in each market (the zeros) come to zero. After the increase in saving there is a decline in planned demand for consumer goods and a negative planned excess demand (or excess supply) appears. To comply with Say's equality there should be a corresponding planned excess demand in one or more of the remaining markets. It is virtually certain that the planned demand will not appear in the labour market. The funds released from consumption expenditure are most unlikely to be used to hire labour. But they could be used to buy capital goods. If so, then I would shift up in figure 6.4 till it intersected with S at some higher level. More probably the excess demand would appear in the bond market. Those who have increased their saving, instead of directly purchasing capital goods, buy bonds, that is, they lend money to firms. This increase in the money lent to firms lowers the interest rate which firms must pay to obtain funds. This in turn will raise I as investment becomes more attractive. Again, the paradox would not be observed.

If the compensating excess demand appears in the money market, however, those who are refraining from spending are then simply accumulating the money in idle hoards (i.e. the velocity of circulation of money is reduced or banks cease to be fully loaned up[3]). Then idle money balances come into being and the paradox of thrift is observed.

FISCAL POLICY

Fiscal policy itself is a two-edged sword. It can involve changes in government expenditure (the G in $C + I + G$) or changes in the level of taxation.

If G is raised then the aggregate demand line is raised and so, in turn, is the equilibrium level of national income (and

---

3. These terms will be explained in Chapters 7 and 8.

vice versa). This, of course, is only true to the extent that government expenditure is *not* funded by money withdrawn from the private sector, otherwise $C + I$ would simply fall by the amount by which $C + I + G$ had been raised. In short, if government intends to raise GNP by increasing expenditure on red tape, neutron bombs, Concorde airliners or whatever, it can only do so by printing the money it needs or by borrowing from overseas lenders who would not otherwise buy British goods.

When taxes are levied C is forced down, since at each level of gross income there is less disposable income and hence less consumption. The amount by which the consumption function declines equals the MPC multiplied by tax taken at that level of income, or vice versa if taxes fall. When taxes are reduced disposable income rises and hence C rises.

For example, assume an MPC of 0.9, an income level of £100 and the imposition of a 10% tax rate. Disposable income falls from £100 to £90 and consumption from £90 to £81 (£10 × 0.9 = £9; £90 − £9 = £81). The effect of such a proportional tax is to make the consumption function flatter along its entire length. A progressive tax rate, where higher incomes pay proportionately more, not proportionately the same, rate of tax, would result in a still further flattening of the consumption schedule. For ease of exposition, neither a proportional nor a progressive tax rate will be used in the following pages, instead lump sum taxes, unrelated to income levels, will be employed. This permits the consumption function to be raised or lowered by the same amount throughout its length as a series of parallel lines.

THE BALANCED BUDGET MULTIPLIER THEOREM

The balanced budget multiplier theorem is, like the paradox of thrift, an attractive theory, but simplistic and so possibly misleading. It states that if all government expenditure is paid for by taxes, then GNP will rise by that amount of expenditure. This is a very tempting piece of economic mumbo-jumbo for politicians and again, like the paradox of

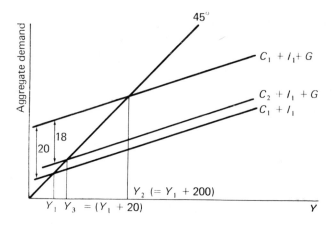

Figure 6.5

thrift, a theory which at first is hard for the businessman or layman to refute.

Consider figure 6.5. At Y_1 no fiscal policy of any kind is in force. Now increase government expenditure from zero to $G = £20$. With a multiplier of 10, Y_1 rises by £200 to Y_2. Now collect taxes of £20 to pay for the G. Disposable income falls by £20, and, with an MPC of 0.9, consumption falls to C_2, a drop of $(0.9 \times £20) = £18$. Now public sector spending equals public sector income. Yet GNP has only fallen to Y_3, £180 below Y_2, given a multiplier of 10.

The net outcome is that, with a balanced budget, GNP can be increased by whatever amount government expenditure is raised by. This theorem is very alluring to politicians who wish to spend more but it assumes that the saving of consumers, now being used to pay 10% of the tax, would *not* have been spent on other things (such as capital goods or bonds). If this was so, if consumer saving had taken the form of idle hoards, then the theorem would be valid. Otherwise, if consumer saving was directly or indirectly being used to purchase capital goods, then government expenditure (even if wholly paid for by the taxes collected from consumers) would merely reduce the I component of $C + I + G$ so that the original GNP level of Y_1 would once again hold.

THE FULL EMPLOYMENT BUDGET

Government fiscal policy generally has as its target a given level of activity in the economy. If the target is 'full employment', namely a situation of 'normal unemployment', then the government's budget will be directed at that goal. An 'expansionary' budget by this definition is not simply one where projected government expenditure exceeds forecasted receipts, but rather it is expansionary if such a deficit is planned *given* normal employment levels as a predetermined target. Conversely a 'restrictive' budget is then regarded as restrictive not simply because estimated government income exceeds estimated G but because such a surplus *will* occur if the 'full employment' target is attained.

Fiscal policy is expansionary if it raises aggregate demand and creates or increases government deficits. It is restrictive if it lowers aggregate demand and removes or reduces government deficits. It is sometimes said that it (fiscal policy) need not even be deliberately employed. There are allegedly built-in stabilisers in the economy which will keep the level of activity close to full employment. For example, if aggregate demand is unexpectedly too high the outcome will be inflation (after some point the only way GNP can rise is if the P component of $P \times Q$ rises). This will be curbed by a fall in G and a rise in taxes (causing a fall in C). G will be less as lower unemployment and other welfare benefits need to be paid out. Taxes will be higher as money incomes rise. As a consequence the whole $C + I + G$ line shifts down and GNP is shifted to the left. Conversely if aggregate demand is too low, the $C + I + G$ line is raised, and GNP is raised in turn by the relevant, multiplied amount. This again occurs automatically as G increases due to rises in unemployment benefits and the like and to falls in the level of tax receipts taken by government.

However, these views may be simplistic. The automatic built-in stabilisers holding down the aggregate demand line may simply result in 'fiscal drag'. In other words private sector expansion may merely be inhibited by the automatic growth of government revenue taken from its income and cash resources. Since it is private sector expansion which generates real economic growth (i.e. enables the Q in the GNP expression $P \times Q$ to grow) this is a dangerous outcome of passive fiscal policy. Equally, in more depressed times, the so-called built-in stabilisers raising G may just, by increasing unemployment benefits, create automatic incentives for people to stay outside the productive labour force, thus perpetuating any recession.

Passive fiscal policy ignores these defects. Active fiscal policy generally ignores the other deficiencies implicit in the paradox of thrift and the balanced budget multiplier theorem. It assumes that tax changes only affect hoards of savings. It assumes that tax changes do not affect bond purchases and that also they do not affect investment. This enables it to employ the following simplistic equation:

$$\Delta \text{ Aggregate demand} = [\Delta G - (\text{MPC})\Delta T] \qquad (3)$$

where T is tax receipts. For example, in figure 6.6, the economy is at $Y_1 = P_1 Q_1$, where Q_1 is not full employment. Nominal GNP of Y_1 could be maintained and real GNP raised to $Y_1 = P_2 Q_f$ where Q_f is full employment output and P_2 is less than P_1. Prices eventually fall (on average) until equi-

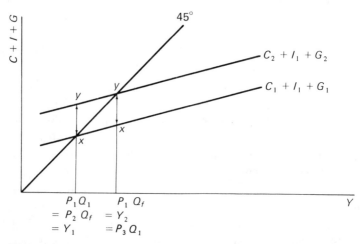

Figure 6.6

librium is attained in each individual market. (As in a movement from Stage 4A to Stage 1 in table 3.2.) But suppose it
is election year and unemployment in a marginal constituency
or throughout the country must be eliminated *now*. The
politicians do not wish to wait for the price mechanism to
operate (even if the economy *could* readjust).

The solution is to raise aggregate demand by the distance
xy and equilibrium GNP will rise to $P_1 Q_f$. The increase xy
can be attained by any combination of ΔG or (MPC) ΔT suggested by equation (3) and by the political expediency of the
moment. (Generally, either will be popular with voters:
government hand-outs *or* tax reductions.) However, apart
from the difficulties already mentioned in this chapter,
proponents of fiscal policy also have the problems of ascer-
taining which is the correct consumption function (the
permanent income time series function, or the cross-sectional
function) since, if an incorrect assumption is made, the
economy may not move to Y_2 as consumption fails to
respond in the way anticipated.

Moreover, the whole notion that adjusting aggregate
demand will somehow increase supply (from Q_1 to Q_f) is
contrary to what any businessman knows to be the truth in
the real world. Wages are paid *before* goods produced are
sold, not afterwards. Putting more money in the hands of
consumers via tax cuts before production increases does not
induce such increases. Increasing government expenditures by
building a new school or road puts money into the hands of
those who built them, but *these* products are not offered for
sale. Again no increase in private sector production is induced
and again the reason is the simple one that *producers* first
require the money to pay the wages to enable the consumers
to buy the relevant (final) goods. The outcome of a rise in
aggregate demand will then be a shift from Y_1 to Y_2 where
$Y_2 = P_3 Q_1$. That is, no change occurs in real GNP, but a
higher money price level exists. Say's principle is not violated,
there is a planned excess demand for money on the part of
producers (to use to hire men and pay their wages) and a
compensating planned excess supply of labour. A rise in the
general price level, inflation, occurs.

Inflation, however, as seen earlier, can be resorted to as a temporary palliative. For as long as this holds true unemployment can be held down *even if economic growth is forfeited.* Growth depends on saving, investment and innovation. Innovation involves change. Change can involve redeployment of resources (including labour) from industry A to industry B. This is unpleasant for some. How much easier (in the short run) to foster inflation, to conceal the signals of price or wage differentials which encourage redeployment (but lose votes). Any remaining unemployment can be blamed on those who hoard money and refuse to invest it in capital goods to produce consumer goods which people do not want. They will refuse because the price differentials between unwanted and wanted goods are so small as to be unattractive. The blame should rather be laid at the door of those who discourage the saving for investment in capital goods for industries which would produce the goods people do want. In short, the true culprits are the workers who refuse to be redeployed, and the politicians who listen to them and who in turn enable or force interest, profits, prices (and wages) to be sufficiently alike in all industries so that capital and labour redeployment is no longer worthwhile.

All these arguments raise the question: 'How *can* governments finance their deficits anyway?' It is to the answer to this question that the next three chapters are devoted. First, the bond market is discussed. Second, the fourth and final macro-market, the money market, is studied. The implicit and simplifying assumption made so far, that changes in the rate of interest which may result from changes in government expenditure, is dropped explicitly. As we saw in our discussion of the balanced budget multiplier, a rise in G need have no effect on Y because of the dampening effect on consumer saving. This was inferred intuitively from Say's equality. It could have occurred due to an initial rise in Y raising interest rates and so reducing the attractiveness of investment and/or the consumption function. This mechanism and its linkages with the Keynesian cross will be explained in the next few chapters.

7
Banking and Monetary Policy

Money has three main functions: it is a medium or facilitator of exchange; it is a unit of account or measure of value; it is a value store. To accomplish these objectives it must be divisible, easily transferable, recognisable and durable (or at least cheap to reproduce). Apart from more esoteric commodities such as shells, cattle and women, a wide variety of objects has served as money over the centuries. Gold has proved one of the more long lasting readily acceptable forms of money. In this chapter money will be defined as notes and coins in circulation (but not notes and coins in bank safes: till money) and current or chequing accounts in banks. Before discussing the banking system, however, we will study the workings of the bond market.

THE BOND MARKET

If governments spend more than they collect in taxes then like any private citizen or firm they must make up the deficit by borrowing. This they do by printing IOUs or government bonds which are sold to the general public (households, firms, commercial banks or overseas equivalents) or to the Bank of England (which in effect means selling them to itself). Here our discussion will be restricted to sales to the public.

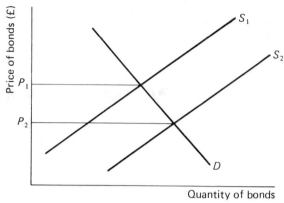

Figure 7.1

What is the effect on aggregate demand of financing budget deficits in this way? Bonds are simply certificates of debt. They have a face or par value which states in pounds what the borrower will pay back on pay-off or maturity day. They also have a coupon interest rate which merely states the amount in pounds the government will pay each year to the holder of the bond. (When the coupon rate is expressed as a percentage it refers to the interest paid on bonds with a face or par value of £100.)

The actual rate of interest (before adjustment from nominal to real for purposes of inflation) depends on the price the owner had to pay for the bond. This, in turn, is determined in the stock market and is unconnected with the par value. Figures 7.1 and 7.2 are two ways of illustrating these statements.

In the bond market (figure 7.1) demand slopes down because lenders receive a fixed payment (the coupon) no matter the price they pay for the bond. The lower the price of the bond, the more attractive this fixed payment becomes. Supply slopes up because issuers of bonds will be more willing to make a promise to provide the fixed coupon payment the higher the price they get for the bond in the first place.

Suppose, on a given trading day in the bond market supply and demand intersect to provide a market price of P_1. The government now decides to issue additional bonds to finance a deficit. Supply increases from S_1 to S_2, by this

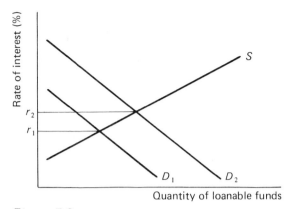

Figure 7.2

new issue of bonds, at each and every price, and to clear this increase in supply the bond price must fall to P_2. However, although coupon rates are unchanged, the actual rate of interest earned by bond holders rises. Consider a bond with a face value of £100. Assume the market price is £50 and the coupon rate is 5%. The government has an obligation to pay £5 per year to the holder of that bond. £5 as a percentage of £50 is 10%: the actual rate of interest. If the market price now fell to £45, the actual rate would rise to £5 expressed as a percentage of £45: namely 11%. Only when bonds sell for their face values are coupon and actual rates identical.

On the other hand, the bond market can be examined (as in figure 7.2) as the market for loanable funds. Here the government is viewed, not as supplying bonds to the public, but as demanding loans from the public. The public are suppliers of the loans. The higher the actual rate of interest, the more willing are the public to supply loans. The lower the rate of interest, the more willing is the government (and others) to borrow.

If the government wishes to fund its deficit it increases its demand for loanable funds at each interest rate. It issues more bonds. Demand rises from D_1 to D_2 and the previous equilibrium interest rate moves up from r_1 to r_2. The rise in interest rate is equivalent to the fall in bond price in figure 7.1. The two are inversely related.

To some extent then, government borrowing to finance

a deficit incurred to push up $C + I + G$ must always be
ineffective. If interest rates rise, I will fall and $C + I + G$ in
turn will drop back. Government borrowing simply 'crowds
out' private sector borrowing and investment spending. How
serious this can be will be discussed in later chapters.

COMMERCIAL BANKS

Commercial banks are institutions that can provide customers
with current accounts against which they can draw cheques.
Most of the nation's money supply is in this form, not in the
form of notes or coin. The money inflows to most banks
seldom exceed their outflows, at least on a short-term basis.
In consequence, banks can lend to householders and firms.
Should their outflows exceed their inflows, then banks
generally hold reserves to guard against such contingencies.

   In fact, although normal commercial prudence would
dictate that the bank should hold reserves, the law also
requires it of them. At present a commercial bank's reserves
should be at least equal to 12½% of its 'eligible liabilities'
(see Note 2, table 7.4). In addition, each bank's average
balance with the Bank of England (part of the 12½%) should
not be less than 1½% of its deposits. These guidelines enable
the government, via the Bank of England, to control the
money supply. First, however, we shall examine in more
detail the concept of fractional reserve banking and how it
permits the commercial banking system as a whole to create
money and so expand the money supply.

FRACTIONAL RESERVE BANKING

Banks operate with reserves of less than 100% of all money
deposited with them. Because they do so they can create
money by lending. Table 7.1 illustrates this process in simplified form. Suppose £1000 is deposited in bank A in a current
account (sight deposits is another name for current or chequing accounts). This £1000 did *not* come from any other

Table 7.1

Bank A (after deposit)

Liabilities		*Assets*		
1. Sight deposits	+ 1000	Reserves		+ 1000
		Required	+ 200	
		Excess	+ 800	

Bank A (immediately after loan)

2. Sight deposits	+ 1800	Reserves		+ 1000
Due to currency	+ 1000	Advance		+ 800
Due to loan	+ 800			+ 1800
		Required	+ 360	
		Excess	+ 640	

Bank A (after loan is spent)

3. Sight deposits	+ 1000	Reserves		+ 200
		Advance		+ 800
				+ 1000
		Required	+ 200	
		Excess	zero	

Bank B (after Bank A's loan is spent)

4. Sight deposits	+ 800	Reserves		+ 800
		Required	+ 160	
		Excess	+ 640	

Bank B (after lending and its own loan is spent)

5. Sight deposits	+ 800	Reserves		+ 160
		Advances		+ 640
				+ 800

The above assumes a 20% reserve requirement.

commercial bank (i.e. it came from either (1) the Bank of England printing more notes or (2) from cash in circulation or (3) the Bank of England buying a government bond from the public, so placing a £1000 Bank of England cheque in the public's hands, or (4) from overseas). Both sides of bank A's balance sheet increase by £1000 as shown.

If it is assumed that there is a legal requirement for a

commercial bank to maintain 20% of its sight deposits as
reserves then initially (stage 1 of table 7.1.) bank A has £800
of excess reserves on the assets side of the balance sheet. On
the assumption that bank A is a profit maximiser it will lend
this money out as soon as possible to borrowers who promise
to give it the highest rate of return. In stage 2 it has done just
that. The £800 has been advanced as a loan, raising the
balance in current accounts to £1800 above the figure they
stood at before the initial injection of £1000. The borrower
has not yet spent the loan, he has merely deposited it in his
newly opened current account. In situation (3) the borrower
has spent his £800 loan and drawn a cheque for that amount
to pay for the goods he has bought. Bank A is now 'fully
loaned up'. It has no excess reserves. The £800 will now be
deposited in the appropriate banks of those who sold goods
to the borrower. Assume all of it is deposited in bank B.
Bank A's loan has become bank B's deposit.

Bank B in turn (situation 4) will find itself with excess
reserves. It can lend out 80% of the £800 of additional
deposits. After it does this, by lending £640, and that loan
in its turn is spent, the situation in stage 5 obtains. Bank B
is now fully loaned up and the process continues as in table
7.2.

Only 80% of each deposit is lent out because of the 20%
reserve requirement. Ultimately the total amount of new
money created equals:

Total of new deposits — original injection of currency
from outside the banks = £4000

Table 7.2 Sight deposits created

Bank	Amount	Source
A	£1000	Deposit of Currency
B	800	Deposit of loan made by A
C	640	Deposit of loan made by B
D	412	Deposit of loan made by C
E	392.6	Deposit of loan made by D
...	...	... ... E
...	...	
...	...	
	£5000	

This can be expressed algebraically. Let x equal the decimal equivalent of the required reserve percentage. Then in table 7.2 each entry equals $(1 - x)$ of the preceding amount. The total amount of money created is given by

$$(1/x \times \text{initial deposit}) - \text{initial deposit}$$
$$= (1/0.2 \times 1000) - 1000 = 4000$$

$1/x$ is called the money multiplier and here equals 5. This can be proved thus:

Total new money (including initial deposit)
= Initial deposit $\times M$ (where $M = 1/x$)
= Initial deposit + Initial deposit $(1-x)$
  + Initial deposit $(1-x)^2$ ...   (1)

Thus

$$M = 1 + (1-x) + (1-x)^2 + \text{to infinity} \ldots \quad (2)$$
$$M(1-x) = (1-x) + (1-x)^2 + (1-x)^3 + \ldots \quad (3)$$

Subtract equation 3 from equation 2

$$M - [M(1-x)] = 1$$
$$M - M + Mx = 1$$
$$M(1 - 1 + x) = 1$$
$$M = 1/x$$

THE BANK OF ENGLAND AND ITS ROLE

The balance sheet of the Bank of England (see table 7.3) has traditionally been subdivided into two parts: one for the Issue Department and another for the Banking Department. The liabilities of the former are mainly notes in circulation and a small amount of notes in the Banking Department. The assets of the Issue Department are composed mainly of British government securities, paid for by printing notes. In the Banking Department this is also the case, although here the securities are bought in another manner. The liabilities in the Banking Department include deposits made by commercial

Table 7.3 The Bank of England: December 1976

Issue Department

Liabilities

Notes in circulation	6858	
Notes in Banking Department	17	£6875 million

Assets

Government securities	5952	
Other securities	923	6875

Banking Department

Liabilities

Public deposits (includes Exchequer)	17	
Special deposits[1]	1806	
Bankers' deposits	325	
Reserves, other accounts and capital[2]	496	£2647 million

Assets

Government securities	1905	
Advances and other accounts	640	
Premises, etc.	84	
Notes and coin	18	2647

1. Deposits called from banks not at their free disposal. The figure was unusually high in 1976. In 1971 it was zero. In most previous years, 1966–1975, it had ranged from £200 to £1400 million.
2. Capital has been constant at £14.6 million.

banks (including, in turn, special and supplementary deposits) and the accounts of government bodies such as the Exchequer and the Paymaster General.

The Bank has several roles. It is the banker to the government. It is also banker to the commercial banks. Both government and commercial banks have accounts with the Bank of England (or central bank) against which they can write cheques. Third, the Bank of England is lender of last resort to the discount market (a role to be examined later) and finally the Bank is the agent of government in a number of subsidiary activities. For example, it controls the money supply, it manages the Exchange Equalisation Account (a government department which holds Britain's gold and foreign currency reserves), and it synchronises inflows and outflows of cash from the commercial banks to the government. This last role will now be examined in more detail since in principle it helps illustrate many of the Bank's other activities.

SYNCHRONISATION OF GOVERNMENT EXPENDITURES WITH CHANGES IN COMMERCIAL BANK RESERVES

The government can add to its account at the Bank of England in two main ways. First, by levying taxes on the public and second, by selling new bonds or securities (or even by selling army surplus).[1] The public then signs cheques payable to the relevant government department. This results in a reduction in the public's deposits at the commercial banks and an increase in government deposits with the Central Bank. The Bank of England then simply makes the necessary bookkeeping changes, increasing the 'public deposits' and reducing 'bankers' deposits' in the balance sheet (see table 7.3 showing the Banking Department's balance sheet and table 7.4 which is a specimen commercial bank balance sheet indicating that that bank has £1 million on deposit at the Bank of England). This alters the money supply (the sight deposits of the commercial banks have fallen). Moreover, the reserves of the commercial banks, as represented by the deposits at the Bank of England, have also fallen. If the commercial banks are fully loaned up this will imply a reduction in their reserves below the legal level and the money multiplier will go to work (this time in reverse as loans are called in and sight deposits increased) thus reducing the money supply still further.

In order to avoid this disruption to the money supply caused by the change in bank reserves and any secondary disruption resulting from the operation of the money multiplier the Bank of England will employ a technique known as 'open market operations'. Where the government is obtaining a net amount of money from the public via tax receipts or sales of new securities, the Bank will buy from the public

---

1. Jack Revell, *The British Financial System*, Macmillan 1975.

Table 7.4 A Commercial Bank's Balance Sheet

Liabilities
Sight deposits	40	
Time deposits	57	
Borrowing from other banks[1] or		
Bank of England	1	
In transmission	1	
Capital	1	£100 million

Assets
Notes and coins	1	1	
Reserve assets[2]			
Balance with Bank of England	1		
Money at call (discount market, other)	5		
Treasury bills	5		
Local authority bills	1		
Commercial bills	1		
Government stock up to 1 year	4	17	
Special[3] and supplementary[4] deposits	2		
Investment (including government stock over 1 year)	20		
Advances	60	82	£100 million

1. The rate of interest charged may be LIBOR (London Inter-Bank Offered Rate), the discount rate, or at the Bank of England's minimum lending rate.
2. Banks are required to maintain 'reserve assets' equal to at least 12½% of their 'eligible liabilities'. 'Eligible liabilities' are sterling deposits (excluding those with an original maturity over 2 years), plus any sterling resources obtained by switching foreign currencies into sterling.
3. Calls for special deposits are expressed as a uniform percentage of each bank's eligible liabilities.
4. Supplementary deposits, sometimes called the 'corset', are non-interest bearing special deposits.

existing government securities to an amount equal to the net income of government. The Bank will write a cheque payable to the public in exchange for the securities. This will increase the public's deposits at the commercial banks by an amount sufficient to offset the original loss. The commercial banks will then present the cheque to the Bank of England which will increase their deposits at the Bank, so restoring their reserve base. Thus the money supply will be restored to its original level and any effect the money multiplier might have had as a consequence of the reserve base change will be nullified.

This example is summarised in table 7.5 where the changes which occur in the balance sheets of the commercial and the Central Bank after the public pays £1000 of taxes to government are shown. If, after situation (a) occurred, the Bank of England did nothing, and the money multiplier was 5, the initial impact would be a reduction in the money supply of £1000 (as shown in the negative £1000 for sight deposits) and the final reduction would be £5000. However, situation (a) is offset by the open market operations implied by stage (b), and stage (c) shows the final outcome. Clearly, the practical effect of stage (c) could be attained in other circumstances as well. For example, if the government wishes to increase its chequing account at the Bank of England by £1000, it merely needs to print and sell a new bond to the Bank for £1000.

Conversely, the reverse procedure will occur if the government makes net positive disbursements to those of the public who do not bank at the Bank of England (e.g. salaries to civil servants, servicemen, National Health Service personnel, suppliers of red tape, local authorities banking with commercial banks, road builders, and so on). The Bank would sell some existing securities from its own portfolio in order to withdraw money from the public's deposits at the commercial banks in order to return these deposits to their original level. This would also ensure that the commercial banks' reserve base of deposits at the Bank of England would in turn remain unchanged.

CONTROL OF THE MONEY SUPPLY

The Bank can control the money supply (i.e. the sum of notes and coins in circulation and of current accounts) in four different ways: by open market operations; by alteration of commercial bank reserve requirements; by influencing interest rates; and by direct regulation.

(a) Open Market Operations
Table 7.5 has already illustrated the use of open market

Table 7.5

Commercial Banks   **Bank of England**

Liabilities	*Assets*	*Liabilities*	*Assets*
Deposits −1000	Balances with Bank of England −1000	Bankers' deposits −1000 Government deposits +1000	

(a) Situation after public pays £1000 in taxes to government.

Liabilities	*Assets*	*Liabilities*	*Assets*
Deposits +1000	Balances with Bank of England +1000	Bankers' deposits +1000	Government securities +1000

(b) Situation after open market operations by Bank of England purchasing securities from public to offset reduction in commercial Bank deposits and reserves.

Liabilities	*Assets*	*Liabilities*	*Assets*
No change	No change	Bankers' deposits: no change Government deposits +1000	Government securities +1000

(c) Situation after open market operations compared to situation before payment of taxes by public.

operations. These involve the purchase or sale of *already issued* government securities without any impact on the total volume of government debt outstanding. In Britain this is a relatively easy matter. First, existing government bonds are by far the most important asset held by the Bank. Second, the value of government bonds in existence (in relation to GNP) is higher in Britain than in any other developed country.[2]

The Bank can buy and sell these bonds in the open market. When it makes a purchase it does so by writing a cheque against thin air. No other firm, individual, government department or commercial bank has this power — each of these has a chequing account somewhere and if any one of them wished to buy a bond (or any good or service) then their deposits with their respective banker (commercial or central) would be correspondingly reduced. The Bank of England, however, has no bank account; it simply writes a cheque against itself (or prints notes) and the cheque or notes are then deposited in the commercial bank of the seller of the security. His current account is increased and the money supply rises and in turn is subject to the money multiplier. When the Bank sells securities the money supply falls.

In practice, it is often difficult to tell when the Bank is conducting open market operations to control the money supply and when it is doing so to synchronise government receipts and expenditures to avoid disrupting commercial bank reserves. *New* issues of government stock, to fund deficits, are generally made on the advice of the Bank. In so far as it overestimates the willingness of lenders to buy them, it will purchase any unsold bills or bonds itself. Thus an activity ostensibly carried out to avoid any impact on the money supply will increase it. Revell,[3] in fact, points out that although new government stocks are issued for public subscription 'in most cases the bulk of the new issues is taken up by organs of the central government (the Departments) and the actual issue to the public is made as they are fed out "on tap" by the Government Broker in the secondary

---

2. Revell, *op. cit.* p. 66.
3. *ibid*, p. 49.

market'. Even this, as will be shown, does not get over the fact that the government, via the central Bank, is simply lending money to itself.

(b) Alterations in Reserve Requirements

Commercial banks cannot create reserves. If they have reserves of £1 million then they can sustain deposits (given a 20% reserve requirement) of £5 million and make loans of £4 million. If the Bank alters the reserve requirement to 25%, the £1 million does not change in absolute terms. But it no longer meets the minimum percentage requirement. Only £4 million of deposits can now be sustained. Borrowers from banks must consequently repay their loans, sell things off in order to do so, or borrow elsewhere. In so doing they receive the money for repayment from existing depositors, thus reducing deposits to £4 million and loans to £3 million.

Simplistically the combined balance sheets of the commercial banks move from situation A to situation B:

(A)

Liabilities		Assets	
Deposits £5		Reserves	£1
		Loans	4
	£5		£5

(B)

Liabilities		Assets	
Deposits £4		Reserves	£1
		Loans	3
	£4		£4

(c) Changes in the Bank Minimum Lending Rate

The Bank can be regarded as lender of last resort to the discount market. Commercial banks lend surplus reserves 'overnight' to the discount houses. Banks with insufficient reserves (relative to the legal minimum) can borrow. Say a bank needs extra reserves now to meet its legal requirements. It can take a government stock to the discount market and get cash for it (which can be deposited at the Bank of England at a discounted (below face or redemption) price). Or it can borrow at a rate of interest equivalent in cost to the discount forgone, had it sold stock. The discount houses have no worries if overnight borrowing and lending are equal in amount. If, however, borrowing from them exceeds lending to them they will be forced to borrow the difference from the Bank of England. This they can do at Minimum Lending Rate. MLR is fixed by administrative decisions. It is not (at least in the first instance) determined by forces of supply and demand in the market place.

Now if this rate is raised unilaterally by the Bank of England the discount houses must pay more for their borrowing. This makes their lending less profitable. They will in consequence raise their lending rates and so increase the cost to banks of borrowing from them. This will in turn reduce the profitability of bank lending, possibly to loss making levels. Banks will therefore either call in loans, rather than borrow to increase their reserves at 'penal interest rates', so reducing the money supply, or, to attain the same objective, they will increase the cost of their own lending, thus resulting in a payment of loans and a reduction of deposits as bank borrowers either borrow elsewhere, or sell things off to other members of the public, in order to repay their bank loans. These other members of the public must make a corresponding reduction in their deposits with the banks to provide the borrowers with the money *they* are using to repay their loans.

The discount houses have one other function worth mentioning here. They purchase by tender the whole of the weekly Treasury bill issue. If they have insufficient funds to do so the Bank will lend them the money (either at MLR or at market rates). Prest and Coppock[4] state 'this is tantamount to the Bank lending directly to the Treasury and so increasing the cash base of the banking system . . .. The danger is that (this) charade hides what is really happening (the printing of money) and so may tend to subordinate monetary policy to the exigencies of government financial needs . . . this may be inflationary'.

(d) Direct Regulation
Finally, the Bank of England can control the money supply through a mixture of direct regulations. One of these is a call

4.   A.R.Prest and D.J.Coppock, *A Manual of Applied Economics*, 5th Edition, Weidenfeld and Nicolson. 1976, p. 67.

for special deposits. These are deposits which must be made by the banks at the Central Bank on demand but which are not defined as reserves. Consequently, if, for example, they must be transferred from the existing reserve base then bank reserves are reduced, the money multiplier goes to work and the money supply is reduced. For example (given a 20% reserve requirement):

All banks before special deposits are called for				*All banks after special deposits are called for*			
Liabilities		*Assets*		*Liabilities*		*Assets*	
Deposits	100	Reserves	20	Deposits	50	Reserves	10
		Other				Special	
		assets	80			deposits	10
						Other	
						assets	30
	£100M		£100M		£50M		£50M

Supplementary deposits are even less attractive to the banks in that they earn zero interest as well as not being included in bank reserves. Unlike special deposits, which tend to work on a once-for-all call-in basis, supplementary deposits operate on a sliding scale (the 'corset'). The higher is the level of a bank's (time) deposits (on which banks pay out interest), the greater is the call for supplementary deposits. This makes the acceptance of time deposits increasingly unprofitable for the banks.

Other direct regulations include qualitative instructions or 'guidance' as to which kind of borrower to favour and which to discourage. For example, export industries often find it easier to obtain loans than do personal borrowers.

In the next chapter we will discuss how all of this affects GNP and in Chapter 9 its relationship with fiscal policy will be examined.

8

Monetary Theory

THE QUANTITY THEORY

The quantity theory of money states that

$$M_s V = PQ = \text{GNP}$$

where M_s is the quantity of money and V its velocity of circulation.

Before the 1930s the predominant view was that prices were solely determined by the quantity of money. Quantity theorists assumed that total physical output and the velocity of money were static, at least in the short run. Irving Fisher[1] argued that 'money is a veil' and that 'the volume of trade, like the velocity of circulation of money is independent of the quantity of money. An inflation of the currency cannot increase the product of farms and factories, nor the speed of trains or ships . . . The whole machinery of production, transportation and sale is a matter of physical capacities and technique, none of which depend on the quantity of money . . . ' So Q was regarded as a constant.

The assumption that V was constant was deemed valid

---

1. Irving Fisher, *The Purchasing Power of Money*, Macmillan 1911, p. 155.

because the rate of turnover of money balances was believed to depend on economic and social relations unaffected by changes in the money supply. Again, to quote Fisher (p.153): 'The average rate of turnover will depend on the density of population, commercial customs, rapidity of transport and other technical conditions, but not on the quantity of money.'

Effectively the early quantity theorists were saying that either $M_s = f(P)$ or $P = f(M_s)$ but not $M_s V = PQ$.

THE NEW QUANTITY THEORY

Two pieces of basic evidence have been produced again and again to refute the early quantity theorists.

First, and most simple to explain, prices have rarely moved in direct proportion to the money supply. For example, in Britain, between 1958 and 1973, M_s expanded nearly four-fold,[2] from £9317 million to £33,431 million. The Retail Price Index, however, only doubled in the same period, from 66.1 to 126.8. Prices and M_s are rarely simply correlated except in very severe inflations.

Second, real GNP, or Q is rarely static even in the short run. And if Q is not static then V cannot be ignored (given the algebraic identity $M_s V = PQ$). To illustrate, consider a four-good economy where each good has a price of £1, where there are two £1 notes and where $M_s V = PQ$. For the four goods to be sold, for the transactions to take place, each of the £1 notes must change hands twice, on average. So $PQ = 1 \times 4 = 4$ and $M_s V = 2 \times 2 = 4$. If for any reason two of the goods rose in price to £1.50, the other two remaining at £1, then if $M_s V$ continued to equal 4 either Q would have to fall, or the prices of the remaining goods would have to drop

---

2.   The money supply is defined here as M_3. In Chapter 7 the quantity of money was defined as circulating cash plus current accounts, M_1. Opinions differ as to how useful this definition is since it excludes deposit accounts, building society deposits and National Savings Bank deposits. These *are* included in M_3. Other forms of 'near money', for example, bearer bonds and plastic credit card facilities are still excluded, however.

(to 0.50p each on average). Normally prices would adjust (although not immediately) but if Q fell, unemployment would occur and effective demand failure might prevent a return to full employment. The early quantity theorists ignored Q in their simplistic equation (and also V) and it was left to Keynes to highlight again the problem of effective demand failure.

In either of these illustrations the injection of Q or V or both into the early quantity theory could have helped explain the observed phenomena. It would have been thought then that Keynes, with his emphasis on effective demand failure, would have quickly embraced the quantity theory as expressed by:

$$M_s V = PQ = \text{GNP}$$

in addition to the Keynesian cross itself, viz:

$$C + I + G = \text{GNP}$$

The fact that he did not was the fault of his early disciples rather than that of Keynes himself. Early Keynesians said that money did not matter. They agreed that, provided the $C + I + G$ multiplier was used correctly, GNP would turn out the way predicted and since $\text{GNP} = M_s V$, then V would take on whatever value was required irrespective of M_s.

Early Keynesians never even considered increases in M_s: they assumed that if it did increase it merely went into idle hoards and so did not affect aggregate demand at all. Correspondingly, V was regarded as some will-o'-the-wisp phenomenon which would automatically fall by the same percentage as M_s rose. Any new money would simply be caught in a 'liquidity trap'. And V would take on whatever value was required for $C + I + G = \text{GNP} = M_s V$ to hold. They also believed, partly as a consequence, that investment spending was chronically weak and so government deficit spending would have to be persistently employed to keep aggregate

demand at the full employment level.[3] In fact, between the
years 1952 and 1976 the United Kingdom did run a persistent
government deficit (or, to put it a different way, a positive
public sector borrowing requirement: PSBR) which ranged
from 2.36% of GDP in 1954 to 11.4% of GDP in 1975. Only
in 1969 and 1970 were tiny surpluses achieved (of 1.18% and
0.04% of GDP respectively).[4]

But *any* level of nominal aggregate demand is sufficient for
full employment provided prices and wages adjust accordingly
— which they do except when abnormal shocks, such as the
Depression, cause effective demand failure. However, the
early income—expenditure analysis of the followers of Keynes
assumed wages and prices were fixed. Thus if nominal aggregate demand declined, unemployment, it was assumed, would
persist until that equivalent — but still nominal — aggregate
demand level was restored.

The prescription[5] was that the Bank should purchase the
government securities printed to fund budget deficits in
whatever quantity was required to keep bond prices high and
interest rates low. This would increase M_s, but this was held
to be of little consequence since V would decrease and
dampen any resulting inflationary effects. The low interest
rates would both encourage investment and facilitate borrowing to finance government spending on the military, red tape,
civil servants, supersonic airliners, social workers or whatever.

However, it became apparent that this prescription did not
work. Large increases in M_s have not been neutralised by
volatile changes in V. Nominal GNP has been increased,

---

3. Keynes himself, according to Leijonhufvud, did not argue in this
    way (cited in A.D. Bain, *The Control of the Money Supply*, Penguin
    1977, p. 85). Nor, according to Sir Dennis Robertson, who quoted
    directly from Keynes, did he go as far as his early disciples with
    these arguments (*Lectures on Economic Principles*, Fontana 1967,
    p. 388).
4. J.M. Buchanan, *The Consequences of Mr Keynes*, Institute of
    Economic Affairs 1978, p. 34.
5. In particular by Hugh Dalton, when as Chancellor (1945—7) he
    attempted to hold nominal interest rates down to 2½%. But the
    policy is still advocated today when low (real) interest rates are
    called for. (Real interest rates approximately equal the nominal
    interest rate minus the rate of inflation.)

inflation has occurred and unemployment has persisted as long as M_s has been ignored. This has led to a rejection of the model that GNP $= C + I + G = M_s V$, where V is an accommodating number which will adjust with M_s to enable the whole three-part equation to hold. Instead attention is now directed towards V itself. This in turn directs our discussion towards the demand for money.

THE DEMAND FOR MONEY

'Liquidity preference' is a phrase often used as a means of expressing the demand for money. Keynes alleged three motives for holding money: transactions, precautionary and speculative.

The transactions motive depends on the level of national income. It governs the demand for money by firms and individuals to fund transactions. The higher is GNP, the higher is this demand. More purchases are being made and paid for. The precautionary motive also depends on the level of national income. It governs how much money will be held to provide for unforeseen contingencies and occasional advantageous purchases. In the following pages we will often lump together these two reasons for holding money.

The speculative motive depends on the relative desires to hold cash or interest-bearing securities. If interest rates on (say) riskless bonds (such as an undated government stock) are high and expected to fall, the stronger will be the desire to hold bonds and not money (since bond prices will be expected to rise); and conversely. Thus this element depends on current and *expected* interest rates.

Now if we return temporarily to algebra we can increase our understanding of liquidity preference and of velocity.

If $M_s V = PQ = \text{GNP}$
then $M_s = Y/V$
             $= Y \cdot K$
where $K = 1/V$

K is a variable dependent on the demand for money, M_D.

The demand for money represents the willingness of people to hold some of their already existing wealth in cash or current accounts, rather than as cars, clothes, bonds or Rembrandts. The smaller is the desire to hold money in liquid form, the lower is K. K is the fraction of national income held as money. That is:

$$M_D = K \cdot Y \tag{1}$$

where Y is nominal GNP and K is a fraction of income depending on liquidity preference. Liquidity preference changes with real interest changes. The higher are real interest rates, the lower is K, and the more willing people are to buy interest-bearing bonds and get out of cash. It also changes with inflationary expectations. The higher are people's expectations with regard to inflation, the keener they are to get out of cash (as a 'precaution') and into goods. K is therefore lower. These two are normally combined or added (real interest rates and inflationary expectations) to obtain nominal interest rates so that equation (1) is written:

$$M_D = K(r) Y$$

where r is nominal interest rates, and K is a function (inverse) of r. (Thus the precautionary and the speculative facets of the demand for money also overlap, just as do the precautionary and the transactions motives, albeit for different reasons.)

A FURTHER EXPLANATION OF VELOCITY

When a person or transactor desires to hold a certain amount of money this does not automatically imply that he wishes to hoard it idly. For example, if the M_D for an individual is found to be £100 per month this is his *average* demand for money over the month. Thus in figure 8.1(a) if £Y represents his month's salary of £200, which he deposits in the bank on

day 1 and then spends at an even rate until on day 15 his
bank balance has fallen to £100 and on day 30 to zero, then
his average daily balance in the bank over the 30 days is
£100. Clearly a transactor can increase (or decrease) the size
of his daily balance by spending more slowly (or rapidly) at
the beginning of the month relative to the end.

In figure 8.1(a) the average balance is $£Y/2$ and the income
velocity of money in the current account is 2 per month (i.e.
income velocity = income/average balance). In figure 8.1(b)
the individual has reduced the average balance held in his
current account by depositing half of his salary in the bank,
and the other half in interest-bearing bonds. The opening
balance in this case is $£Y/2$ and this declines at a steady rate
to zero in the middle of the month. At this point the individual
must redeem his bonds and deposit the proceeds in the bank
if he is to maintain the same expenditure pattern as figure
8.1(a). His average daily balance, however, has been reduced
to $£Y/4$ by this temporary use of one half of each month's
income to purchase bonds and the income velocity of money
rises to 4 per month (income/average balance = 4). Or, in
terms of K, K has fallen in these examples from ½ to ¼.

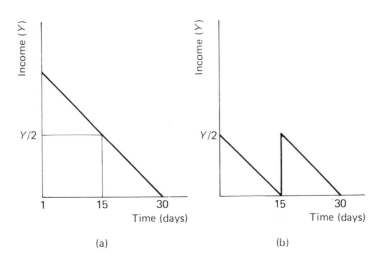

Figure 8.1

EQUILIBRIUM IN THE MONEY MARKET

Figure 8.2 shows one way of determining equilibrium in this, the fourth and final macro-market. M_s is what the Bank of England says, thus it is drawn as a horizontal line. (To the extent that the commercial banks are not fully loaned up because their lending confidence is low when GNP is low, then it would slope up slightly to the right.) For any given interest rate (r) equilibrium is at e_1, or GNP level Y_1.

Since $M_D = K(r)Y$, then if r does not change, K will be a constant fraction, and as Y rises M_D will rise in direct proportion (M_D is the transactions demand for money embracing also some element of the precautionary motive). Equilibrium is at e_1 since there the supply of money which exists equals the money that some people somewhere are and must be willing to hold. At that point, Y_1 is the nominal GNP level that makes the aggregate money that all transactors hold equal the actual quantity of money in existence. At a point such as f there would be excess demand for money of $e_2 f$. Transactors, households and firms would attempt to add to their bank or cash balances. But since M_s is fixed each and every transactor cannot do this. In an attempt to hold money equal to $Y_2 f$ in aggregate, transactors cut back on expenditures; GNP thus falls (either the P or the Q component) until Y_1

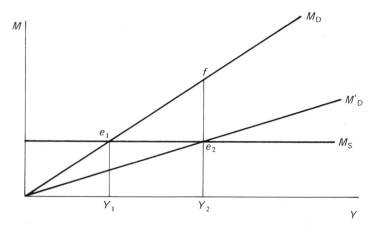

Figure 8.2

is reached. To the left of e_1, $M_s > M_D$. Transactors in aggregate hold more money than they wish. They increase their spending to reduce their cash balances and GNP rises to Y_1.

If the interest rate is increased, K falls, and M_D also falls. Velocity rises and, in figure 8.2, M_D pivots to M'_D. A new equilibrium GNP of e_2, Y_2 is established. The money supply has not changed. The existing supply of money is simply circulating more rapidly.

In the following chapter an attempt is made to synthesise the two policies, fiscal and monetary, and the four macro-markets are also formally brought together for the first time.

9
Synthesis

In this chapter all four macro-markets (bonds, commodities or goods, labour and money) are linked together in an analytic whole. The material of preceding chapters is brought together and synthesised. The linkages between fiscal policy and monetary policy are explained. The weaknesses of simplistic fiscal policy are highlighted, particularly its underestimation of the role of interest rates, and so of the money and bond markets. One reason for this is that fiscal policy, *qua* fiscal policy, is only possible if, in funding a deficit, the government does *not* sell bonds to the Bank of England. If, as generally happens, the Central Bank *does* buy bonds from the government, the result is the equivalent to the printing of further fiat money.[1] The money supply is then increased and the money market is affected. If, conversely, the bonds are sold to the public, interest rates rise as bond prices fall. In this case the money supply may remain invariant, but the demand for money (as was seen in Chapter 8) may change for precautionary and speculative reasons. If this demand change does not involve a velocity change also, however, fiscal policy can be both ineffectual and indeed counter-productive.

---

1. Fiat money is money with no intrinsic value (unlike gold or silver). It is accepted on trust or by faith in the belief that it will be readily accepted as a means of exchange.

The following pages explain these factors in detail, show how any conflicts may be reconciled (as some claim) and explain why some monetarists believe, in fact, that such reconciliation is not feasible.

THE DIRECT AND INDIRECT MECHANISMS

Both mechanisms can be analysed either diagrammatically or with the aid of a Say's principle table. Consider first the direct mechanism (table 9.1 and figure 9.1). This ignores the bond market and looks only at commodities.

Suppose the Bank of England raises the money supply (by, for example, changing reserve requirements) to M_s' in figure 9.1. In table 9.1 this E_S is immediately reflected by an E_D in the commodity market. GNP would rise until general equilibrium in all four markets was reattained.

Diagrammatically Y_1 ceases to be the equilibrium nominal GNP which now becomes Y_2. In the money market trans-actors try to get rid of their excess money balances. This results in more expenditure reflected in either or both a higher P or Q. In the commodities market extra C or I is generated, or even some local government expenditure to the extent that it is funded by commercial banks.

The indirect mechanism assumes that changes in M_s affect the commodity market *via* changes in the rate of interest. When r changes that causes the $C + I + G$ line to shift. This is illustrated both in table 9.2 and figure 9.2.

Open market purchases of bonds by the Bank raise the price of bonds from P_1 to P_2 This results in M_s rising to M_s'. However, the bond price rise also pushes down the interest rate so M_D pivots up to M_D' in the money market [$M_D = K(r)Y$ and K is inversely related to r] as people's liquidity preference rises. However, more money is now available at each income level than before and the economy moves (in the money market) from e_1 to a to b to e_2 and (in the commodity market) from e_1 to b to e_2, resulting in the new, higher, equilibrium nominal GNP of Y_2.

Table 9.1

	Bonds	*Labour*	*Commodities*	*Money*
General equilibrium	0	0	0	0
Money supply raised	0	0	E_D	E_S
GNP rises	0	0	0	0

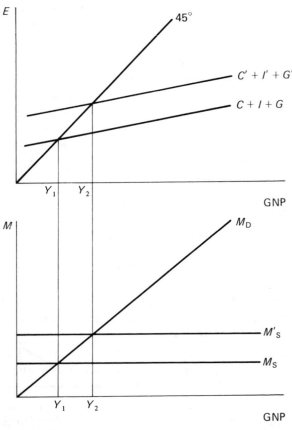

Figure 9.1

Table 9.2 Indirect linkage between the money and commodity markets

			Bonds	Commodities	Money
(1)	GE	e_1	0	0	0
(2)	$\uparrow M_s$	a	E_D	0	E_S
(3)	$\downarrow r$	b	$0(e_2)$	E_D	E_S
(4)	$\uparrow Y(\text{GE})$	e_2	0	0	0

(1) General equilibrium
(2) Open market purchases
(3) Bond prices rise, interest rates (nominal and real) fall. Equilibrium is re-established in bonds. M_D pivots to M'_D.
(4) C and I shift up. I is cheaper, S is less attractive, desire to get out of cash into goods.

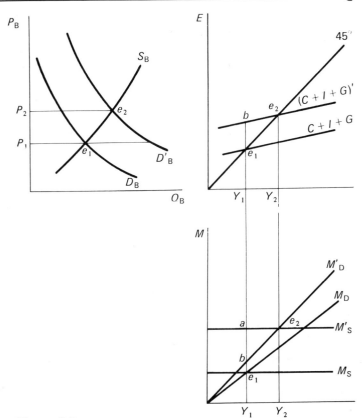

Figure 9.2

Table 9.3

	Bonds	Commodities	Money
GE	0	0	0
$\uparrow M_s$	E_D	E_D	E_S
$\downarrow r$	0	E_D	E_S
$\uparrow Y$(GE)	0	0	0

Table 9.3 illustrates how the direct and indirect mechanisms could work together when M_s is increased.

IS FISCAL POLICY POSSIBLE?

To the extent that a budget deficit or surplus even inadvertently affects the money supply then the economic policy in question must be a mixed and not a purely fiscal one. Its forecasted impact should then be gauged by any effect emerging from the two policies combined.

When is a pure fiscal policy possible? Consider a fiscal policy deficit which results in a public sector borrowing requirement (PSBR) which must be financed by sales of government bonds. A pure fiscal policy results if the bonds are sold directly to the public at large. If the bonds are sold to the Bank of England, however, the policy is both fiscal and monetary simultaneously. Table 9.4 shows the impact on the balance sheet of the commercial banks and that of the Bank of England if £1000 of new bonds are sold to the public. First, the public reduces its deposits in order to pay for the bonds. The Bank of England receives the public's cheque and increases the government's deposits with it by £1000, and offsets this by deducting £1000 from the commercial banks' balances at the Bank of England. This in turn reduces the commercial banks' reserves by £1000. In stage 2 of table 9.4 the government now spends the £1000 to buy the red tape, pay the social workers, subsidise Concorde or whatever is implicit in its deficit. The £1000 cheque written out by government is deposited in the commercial banks, who in turn present it to the Bank of England, which increases their

Table 9.4

Stage 1

Commercial Banks				*Bank of England*	
Liabilities		*Assets*		*Liabilities*	*Assets*
Deposits	− £1000	Reserves	+ £1000	Government deposits + £1000 Bank deposits − £1000	

Stage 2

Liabilities		*Assets*		*Liabilities*	*Assets*
Deposits	+ £1000	Reserves	− £1000	Government deposits − £1000 Bank deposits + £1000	

deposits there (and so their reserves) by £1000 and reduces the government's balance by £1000. Commercial bank deposits are unchanged by the operation. The entries are exactly offsetting. The policy is purely fiscal in nature. The converse would apply if a government surplus was budgeted for. Current account deposits would be unaltered, the money supply unchanged.

When the government sells new bonds to fund a deficit to the Bank of England (or to the discount market financed by loans from the Bank of England) then the policy *does* have an impact on the money supply. Table 9.5 shows how the Bank of England buys the new securities by writing a cheque against thin air. Government deposits in stage 1 are increased by the £1000 paid to the respective government departments by the Bank. The asset side of the Bank's balance sheet is increased by the new securities. In stage 2 the government spends the £1000 on red tape, Concorde airliners, etc. and the suppliers of goods or labour to these activities deposit their cheques in the commercial banks. The commercial banks present the cheque to the Bank of England, which increases their deposit by £1000 and reduces those of government by

Table 9.5

Stage 1

Bank of England

Liabilities	*Assets*
Government deposits + £1000	Government securities + £1000

Stage 2

Commercial Banks		*Bank of England*	
Liabilities	*Assets*	*Liabilities*	*Assets*
Deposits + £1000	Reserves + £1000	Government departments	− £1000
		Commercial banks	+ £1000

£1000. This in turn increases commercial bank reserves. The money supply has now been increased by £1000. Commercial bank deposits have risen by £1000. So, of course, have commercial bank reserves. Thus the money supply will now rise still further as the money multiplier goes to work and the commercial banks lend out their surplus reserves. (Note: although the banking system can multiply reserves, it cannot create them in the first instance, only government activity can do that.)

If government spends more than it collects in taxes (which it invariably does) and it pays for the difference by selling bonds directly or indirectly to the Bank, it is exactly the same thing as printing more money to pay for the difference. It is difficult to ascertain exact figures, but the size of the Bank's holdings of government securities arouse more than a suspicion that British government deficits are financed in large part by the printing press.

DOES FISCAL POLICY WORK?

Pure fiscal policy only occurs if, when deficits (or surpluses)

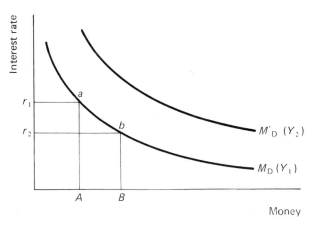

Figure 9.3

are run, the government sells (buys) new securities to (from) the public and not to the Bank of England.

If fiscal policy is to be effective and M_s constant then, in the equation $M_s V = PQ = \text{GNP}$, V must change if GNP is to change. Does V change with fiscal policy amendments? To answer this, demand for money lines must again be examined. The *transactions* demand line has already been used (e.g. in figure 8.2) where, with a given r, M_D varied according to the level of GNP. The same information can be contained in a diagram like figure 9.3 which contains two *speculative* demand for money lines. Each of these lines shows the demand for money given a level of GNP but varying r. Which diagram is more suitable depends simply on the variable one wishes to emphasise. (M_D' indicates a higher demand for money than M_D, given that $Y_2 > Y_1$.)

Velocity is higher at a than at b since GNP is steady at Y_1, but M_D is only A in the former and B in the latter case. Fewer pounds finance the same money income at A than at B. Algebraically

$$V = Y_1/A \quad \text{or} \quad Y_1/B \quad \text{and} \quad Y_1/A > Y_1/B.$$

In short, velocity's variability depends on the nature of M_D. So whether or not fiscal policy can work depends on the potential for variability of V and so, in turn, of M_D.

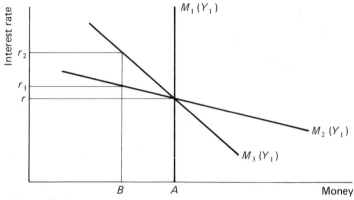

Figure 9.4

Consider figure 9.4. Three different money demand lines are shown. (Only the *nature* of the lines differ, not their magnitude, i.e. $M_1 = M_2 = M_3$.) Each is also drawn for the same GNP, Y_1. If M_D lines look like M_1 then V does not vary under any circumstances. Irrespective of the level of r, $V = Y_1/A$. Conversely if M_D lines look like M_2 then V varies considerably with changes in the interest rate. For example, for V to change from Y_1/A to Y_1/B requires only an interest rate change from r to r_1. With M_D lines with properties like those of M_3, a similar V change could only be induced by a change in r from r to r_2.

So fiscal policy, even if possible, will not be very effective, if at all, with money demand lines like M_1. Conversely it will be effective if they are shaped like M_2.

HICKS—HANSEN AND FRIEDMAN

The Hicks—Hansen version of the monetary—fiscal synthesis is slightly more complex than the above.[2] Named after the economists who first derived it, the Hicks—Hansen synthesis is a model which embraces the interacting effects of interest and investment, interest and money, and the fiscal and monetary approaches to income determination.

---

2. This section can be omitted by readers following highly compressed courses.

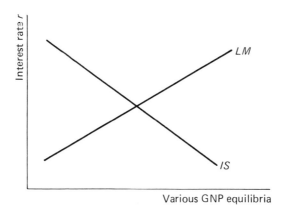

Various GNP equilibria

Figure 9.5

Figure 9.5 shows their synthesis in skeletal form. The *IS* line considers only those combinations of *r* and GNP which equate investment and saving (i.e. equilibrium GNPs and the corresponding interest rates when $I = S$). Figure 9.6 shows how *IS* can be derived. Figure 9.6(a) shows how *I* rises from I_3 to I_1 as *r* falls from r_3 to r_1, all other things equal. Figure 9.6(b) shows the corresponding Keynesian crosses for the three different *I* levels brought about by the interest rate changes. *C* and *G* remain constant at C_0 and G_0 respectively. And since saving equals investment at Y_1, Y_2 and Y_3, the *IS* line can be plotted for each of the GNP levels which resulted from the relevant interest rates (figure 9.6(c)).

Obviously *IS* slopes down. Will the slope be gentle or steep? It will slope down more steeply if the marginal efficiency of investment, and so investment itself, does not respond much to interest rate changes, and vice versa. That is, if for any given fall in *r*, the increase in investment is small, then the multiplied increase as it affects *Y* must also be absolutely small. This will be so irrespective of the size of the multiplier. Secondly, *IS* will slope more steeply, the lower is the MPC. Geometrically, the flatter is $C + I + G$, the less will be the movement along the GNP axis for any given vertical addition of *I* to the aggregate demand line. Algebraically, the multiplier will be smaller the lower is MPC.

But *IS* only shows a range of equilibrium GNPs in the commodities and labour markets. The actual GNP will depend

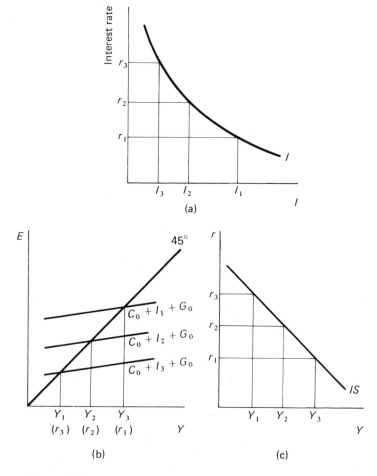

Figure 9.6

on the equilibrium rate of interest. This will be determined in the bond and money markets. The *LM* line in figure 9.5 shows those combinations of r and GNP which equate liquidity preference (M_D) and a given M_s.

Figure 9.7(a) depicts such a given M_s. It is not drawn vertically, on the assumption that banks are not fully loaned up at lower interest rates. (Figure 9.7(c) shows the same given M_s on a transaction demand for money lines diagram rather than a speculative demand for money lines diagram as in figure 9.7(a). The results are identical.) When interest rates

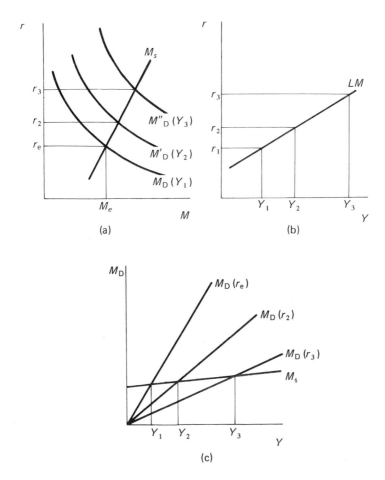

Figure 9.7

are low banks are less willing to lend, economic activity is also generally lower and so lending is riskier and less attractive. (Compare M_s on figure 9.7(c).)

Knowledge of how supply and demand curves operate, particularly in the money and bond markets, explains why M_e and r_e indicate the equilibrium interest rate for GNP level Y_1. But as soon as different levels of GNP are considered and M_D moves out to M'_D or M''_D for Y_2 and Y_3 respectively, different rates of interest represent the equilibrium rate. Similarly, in figure 9.7(c), falling interest rates result in a rise, or a pivoting to the right, of M_D, the transactions demand for money. New equilibrium GNP levels then hold. From either of these graphs figure 9.7(b), the *LM* line, can then be plotted.

The *LM* line slopes up, reflecting the notion that higher GNPs result in higher interest rates, given the money supply, as M_D increases. Is the slope steep or gentle? It will slope more steeply, the steeper is the M_D curve of figure 9.7(a). (Recall figure 9.4, where velocity did not change appreciably on money demand curve M_2 for the same GNP given a change in the interest rate.)

A much larger change in r is thus required to move from any given GNP level to a given higher one if M_D is steep rather than gentle. In geometric terms, for any given shift in M_D *horizontally*, at each and every point (including equilibrium) on figures 9.7(a) and 9.7(c) the new equilibrium r *must* be much higher if M_D has a relatively steep slope. The slope of M_s also affects the slope of *LM*, but since M_s is presumed near to vertical in most cases anyway this is probably of less import (i.e. banks are presumed to be generally fully or close to fully loaned up).

The situation where $IS = LM$ shows where all four macro-markets are simultaneously in equilibrium. An increase in M_s will move *LM* down and to the right, lowering r and raising the equilibrium GNP. Expansionary fiscal policy will move *IS* up to the right raising r at each GNP equilibrium. Figures 9.8(a) to 9.8(d) show respectively situations where the shapes and positions of the two curves render monetary policy and fiscal policy ineffective, and also where fiscal and monetary policies are apparently potent instruments. (Note the relative gaps between Y_1 and Y_2 when *LM* shifts to *LM'* and *IS* to *IS'*.)

Samuelson argues that the debate between Keynesians and Monetarists boils down to this: an argument over the respective shapes of the *IS* and *LM* curves.[3] Chicago's Milton

3. P.A. Samuelson, *Economics*, 10th Edition, Prentice-Hall 1977.
4. Cited from W. Peterson, *Principles of Macro Economics*, 3rd edition, Irwin 1977.

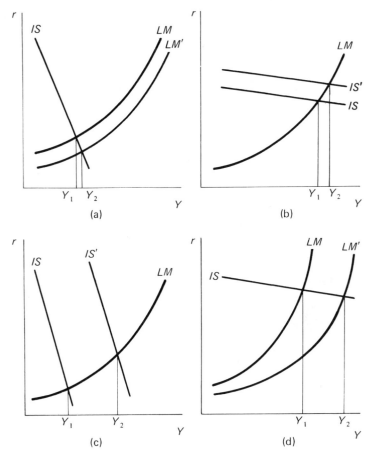

Figure 9.8

Friedman, however, says the differences are much more fundamental.[4] First, he believes in a *consistent* growth of M_s, not a varying one. Governments can be misled by economic statistics (e.g. see the discussion on permanent income above) and so are likely to choose the wrong policy at the wrong time, or the wrong variation in the variable chosen. So governments are destabilisers of the economy. In short, monetarists do *not* argue for an active monetary policy, but rather a *passive and predictable* one. 'Fine tuning' is seen as accomplishing the reverse, irrespective of the policy adopted.

Second, Friedman points out that changes in M_s change r

in the *IS:LM* model. This is accomplished in the bond market, and so investment and GNP are altered. However, Friedman argues that raising M_s can increase people's money holdings above what they would wish. This may indeed result in the prediction of the *IS:LM* model. But people are *not* limited to bonds or capital goods when they try to dispose of their money. They may instead buy cars, clothes, holidays or other things *immediately*, before any extra spending power raises investment and so the $C + I + G$ line which permits them to raise their consumption *ultimately*. As a consequence changing M_s may be much more potent than it is in either the simplistic Keynesian model where the 'paradox of thrift' and 'balanced budget multiplier' rule supreme, or in the *IS:LM* model where 'money does matter' but *intially* any increase is channelled into capital investment directly or indirectly via bonds. If the increase in M_s goes *immediately* into C or G then the result is simply inflation — or 'too much money chasing too few goods'.

Friedman[5] goes on to argue that inflation is simply a tax since as incomes rise (given progressive taxation) tax income rises still faster *without* legislation (fiscal drag). This, of course, makes inflation popular with governments since it is (apparently) a painless way of raising the income to pay for any government expenditure which will be popular with important sections of the electorate. Inflation, however, hurts the private citizen as a taxpayer. It harms those who do not wish for the expenditures in question but who must pay for them, it harms lenders since they are ultimately to be paid back in depreciated currency, and it hurts those on fixed incomes whose purchasing power consequently falls (e.g. widows, orphans, pensioners). It also distorts the relative prices in the market place, making it more difficult for trans- actors to negotiate optimal trades since their information about each other's preferences expressed in pounds is that much less reliable.

However, inflation does benefit borrowers since loans are

---

5. See, for example, Milton Friedman, *Monetary Correction*, Institute of Economic Affairs 1974.

paid back in yesterday's pounds (the biggest borrower of all is, of course, government). And it benefits those who obtain the extra money first; *before* prices have risen. Since the additional money originates in the government's printing presses government is again the main beneficiary of inflation. (Once the new currency has worked its way through the economy to private individuals its purchasing power will have fallen, money prices will have risen.) The analogy with the criminal money counterfeiter is obvious. The counterfeiter who can get rid of his false money benefits; so do his immediate suppliers of goods and services. But if velocity remains unchanged, the injection of counterfeit money will in the long run simply raise money prices. The final recipients of the false money in any period and/or those unable to negotiate increased money incomes to compensate for the rising money prices will simply suffer a reduced living standard.

Buchanan[6] further argues, bolstering Friedman's views, that governments will rarely use fiscal policy as Keynes intended anyway. Persistent deficit financing will be employed to purchase power and votes, rather than to stabilise the economy. As we have seen, budgetary surpluses are both rare and insignificant in size.

CROWDING-OUT

Fiscal policy involves movement of the $C + I + G$ line on the Keynesian cross diagram with (in the near universal case of deficit budgeting) sales of bonds to the Bank of England or the general public. Only in the latter case does the money supply not rise. Given sales of bonds to the public, the price of bonds will fall and r will rise. This will shift downwards both the C and I components of the $C + I + G$ line. If velocity does not change (M_1 type demand line as in figure 9.4) and if M_s is unchanged then GNP will be unaltered. Public sector borrowing will have completely 'crowded-out' private sector borrowers and investors. G will rise, but $C + I$ will fall by a fully compensating amount.

---

6. Buchanan, *op. cit.*

Had the expansionary policy been a reduction in taxes and not a G increase, $C + I + G$ would rise but the deficit would still require the sale of bonds, again pushing up r if the sale is to the public. $C + I$ would again revert to their original situation, since neither V nor M_s would have changed. Tax cuts, unless accompanied by cuts in government expenditure, or velocity or money supply increases, cannot increase nominal GNP under such circumstances.

If money demand lines are near horizontal (like M_2 in figure 9.4) crowding-out is no problem. Pure fiscal policy deficits can be funded by selling bonds, r can rise, but the rise will be small and the increase in velocity will be great. Private transactors will take money out of idle balances to lend to government. If government did not borrow them, they would remain in the 'liquidity trap', no private investor would use them. Moreover, the change in r is so slight that the private sector is not induced to cut back on either C or I. This is the simple Keynesian multiplier model where V is a will-o'-the-wisp taking on whatever value is required, and capable of expanding substantially at the slightest provocation.

More probably money demand lines will be like M_3 in figure 9.4 and neither zero nor total crowding-out will be a problem. The issue will be one rather of degree.

10
Stagflation and the Business Cycle

What prescription can be written for an economy suffering simultaneously from inflation and recession? Expansion or contraction will merely intensify the problem. Some will argue that the problem can be solved by actively discouraging foreign trade since, on their view, the inflation is 'imported' in the form of higher and higher prices for goods purchased abroad. Others would argue for a strict wages policy to curb the power of those trades unions who demand ever higher wages which results (in their view) in ever higher prices. Neither of these positions has been adopted in this book. Rather the fact that information is not free has been stressed (in the discussion on the Phillips Curve, in the observation that prices are rarely the first economic variables to move and so on).

HAYEK ON STAGFLATION [1]

F.A. Hayek argued that inflation could only temporarily reduce unemployment. Like Friedman's view of the expectations-adjusted Phillips Curve, Hayek's explanation is also based on the fact that transactors only have imperfect information

---

1. See F.A. Hayek, *The Constitution of Liberty*, Routledge and Kegan Paul 1977, pp. 330–333, and Baird, *op. cit.*, pp. 84–85.

(but he does not focus on the job search process). The allocation of resources in an economy is a complex task. It is inevitable that mistakes will be made, whether the economy is
controlled by the market or by a command mechanism (see
page 2). Either individual businessmen or the central planner
could fail to perceive consumers' wants correctly. Information
costs, however, are much lower in the exchange economy
because individual entrepreneurs need only concern themselves with those data relevant to the particular markets in
which they are operating. In a centrally planned economy, all
information must be collected and collated and analysed
simultaneously in one place. In either situation mistakes will
be made.

For example, labour can be drawn into jobs where there is
insufficient demand for the final product to pay wages. In a
decentralised economy this normally becomes quickly
apparent. Firms which overestimated the demand for their
product will fail and the workers employed there will seek
out better (consumer supported) jobs.

However, during unanticipated inflation, even firms making
products for which there is insufficient demand will prosper.
This is because employers are able to hire workers at a given
wage rate which is low compared to the price of the final
product when it is eventually sold. Indeed, both worker and
employer are probably unaware that the wage rate agreed on
is low in comparison with what the price of the final product
will become.

If the demand for the final product, however, is such that
in the absence of inflation the selling price is neither what the
employer originally expected, *nor* a higher money figure, but
is a figure lower than both of these, then the firm's expected
profit is either less than anticipated or is a loss. The firm
would then cut back on employment or even go out of
business. With unanticipated inflation, however, the originally
hoped for selling price, or more, can be obtained, and labour
will continue to be employed. However, as soon as workers
anticipate the inflation they will cease to be content to work
for the original (and now relatively low) money wage. The
temporary profits created by the inflation will vanish, and

firms producing products for which there is insufficient actual demand will cut back on employment or go out of business.

Inflation (as in the Phillips curve analysis) can temporarily reduce unemployment by postponing the time when misdirected labour will be laid off. It is always ultimately necessary to fire workers where there is insufficient real demand for what their labour produces. The deficiency in demand may be because of a change in taste by consumers or errors in judgement by businessmen. In either case, inflation makes it more difficult to perceive the actual lack of demand and postpones the inevitable reallocation of resources which must occur.

This argument only holds, as stated, if the inflation is unanticipated. Transactors can adjust their behaviour to the market's real needs if the inflation is anticipated. As a corollary, only a continuously accelerating rate of inflation can indefinitely postpone the inevitable unemployment (the stagflation) which will emerge when the misdirected labour begins to look for jobs that can be supported by the actual pattern of demands.

THE BUSINESS CYCLE

Although changes are continually taking place in the economy — some industries are growing, some declining — why should there ever be a *general* boom or slump? The only phenomenon which permeates the whole economy is money and it is to this we must look for an answer and explanation. Why should rises or falls in the demand for or supply of money generate the business cycle?

The main problem is why is there suddenly a *'cluster'* of business errors? Businessmen and entrepreneurs are market experts (otherwise they would not survive) and why should they all make mistakes simultaneously? A secondary issue is why do capital goods industries fluctuate more widely than consumer goods ones? And a third question is why does the quantity of money rise in a boom and fall in a slump?

The business cycle is generated by monetary expansion

and contraction.[2] Assume the money supply is constant. People will have a *time preference*. The less consumption they prefer now, the lower will be their time preference, and the lower the 'pure interest rate'. The proportion of income devoted to saving and investment will be higher and the capital stock of the economy will be built up, lengthening the production process as the division of labour increases. Higher time preferences will have the reverse effect. The final market rate of interest will reflect the pure interest rate plus or minus the relevant entrepreneurial rewards and inflation rate.

When new money is printed it appears as if the supply of savings has increased. Interest rates fall and businessmen are misled into borrowing additional funds to finance extra investment activity. This investment occurs first in capital goods industries rather than consumer goods ones. The 'process of production' is lengthened. This would be of no consequence if it had been the outcome of a genuine fall in time preferences — it could be sustained indefinitely — but the change was government induced. The new money reaches factor owners in the form of wages, rent and interest. Given unchanged time preferences, the factor owners will then spend the higher money incomes in their existing consumption: investment proportions. That is, demand will move back from the higher orders to the lower orders of production (to industries closer to the final consumer). Capital goods industries will find their expansion has been in error and malinvestments have been incurred. Losses will be made due to entrepreneurial misjudgements and the malinvestments must somehow be liquidated. In short, 'booms' of this type are wasteful misinvestment due to government interference with the market place. The 'crisis' occurs when consumers attempt to re-establish their desired consumption—income proportions. The ensuing 'depression' follows as night follows day. It is simply the process of adjustment which the economy makes to correct the errors and the wastes of the boom. It continues until consumer demands are efficiently met once again.

---

2. The explanation given here relies on Ludwig von Mises', *Human Action*, Regnery 1966.

'Depression' is the necessary and inevitable 'recovery' process of a government-induced boom.

Just as the boom was marked by a fall in the rate of interest, so it was characterised by a bidding-up of the prices of industrial goods relative to those of the consumer goods and of commodity prices relative to those of industrial goods. So the depression sees a fall in all prices with those furthest from the consumer falling fastest. As factors shift back to the lower orders of production some natural unemployment will occur. This will disappear provided real wage rates are not artificially high.

Such price movements need only be relative, however. Hence the problem of stagflation — a slump with rising money prices. If government keeps on injecting money into the economy the adjustment between capital and consumer goods industries will still proceed. Hence the prices of consumer goods still rise relatively in a slump, but do so monetarily and absolutely as well. Government, by intervening in the economy's recovery process from the government-induced slump, has now 'deprived the public of the one great advantage of recessions: a falling cost of living'.[3] Not only that, but the recovery will be delayed. One of the most insidious effects of inflation is that it disguises price signals. Absolute price differentials are difficult enough for entrepreneurs (businessmen or consumers) to perceive but changes in the rates of price change, when most are changing and that upwards, given the countless goods involved, blur the signals of the market and so the wishes of consumers to the detriment of their fulfilment.

Nonetheless the money supply *does* tend to fall in a slump, if only relative to what it would have been without government intervention. The reason is that banks tend to call in loans and be less willing to lend. In short, the money multiplier falls. Moreover, if prices are falling, people's time preference rises and the demand for money increases. They wish to hold cash instead of goods.

---

3. Murray Rothbard, *America's Great Depression,* Sheed and Ward 1971 (Introduction).

Rothbard[4] suggests that the ways *not* to move out of a depression rapidly are for government to do the following:

(1) delay liquidations by aid to ailing firms,
(2) have further monetary expansion so delaying adjustment and worsening the current malinvestment 'clusters',
(3) maintain real wages so worsening unemployment,
(4) maintain prices so preventing (a) return to low price prosperity if a floor is imposed or (b) a reduction in real wages in non-productive sectors if a ceiling is placed on prices,
(5) stimulate consumption and so discourage saving and investment (thereby falling into the traps of the so-called paradox of thrift and the balanced budget multiplier theorem).
(6) subsidise unemployment by 'job creation' schemes and high unemployment benefits so delaying the transfer of labour to where the jobs are available and the output wanted by consumers.

This theory of the business cycle, as propounded by Mises, and later by Hayek, assumes neither initial full employment nor over-investment. The assumptions are rather that inflation misdirects labour and capital resources. The malinvestment may or may not be 'better' than unemployment, but irrespective of the latter's existence or otherwise, complementary factors, already in employment, will be diverted into working with them with all the corresponding distortions, wastes and succeeding slump.

The Austrian theory (Hayekian and Misesian) is the only business cycle theory which incorporates the cycle into the general corpus of economics. The notion of 'over-production' for one, does not explain why *all* entrepreneurs (market experts) malinvest simultaneously. The Austrian view is that there is over- and under-production in different sectors. The converse idea of 'under-consumption' is essentially the

4. *ibid.*, page 26.

Keynesian notion of inadequate aggregate demand. It rests on concepts of over-saving and under-investment. Yet as Sir Dennis Robertson pointed out, this suggests that Keynesians decide first how much income to consume and not to consume (i.e. save) and, second, how much of these savings should be hoarded and how much invested. They are incapable of 'visualising more than two margins at once'.[5] But all individuals allocate their income into these three different channels simultaneously according to their time preferences (thus determining spending on present and future consumption) and utilities of money (thus determining the level of their cash balances). Investment requires consumption restriction and the saving of funds. The two words, on this view, are almost interchangeable. Moreover, 'unplanned' investment (positive or negative) in the Keynesian model is universal, yet no explanation is given as to why the implied cluster of errors should be made simultaneously by the entrepreneurial market experts. Surely many will not make mistakes, and many who do will reduce prices so boosting consumption? And again, if 'unintended' investment is valid either as a theory or an outcome then it will, by the under-consumptionist view, be in the consumer goods industries where inventories will pile up. Yet empirically this is not so. Capital goods industries are more cyclically prone! Mises explains that crises are marked by malinvestment and under-saving, not by under-consumption.

Similarly, the acceleration principle described earlier, although attractive, does not fit the error clustering of the business cycle. Nor does it take account of supply and demand. If demand rises for one good, it will fall for another. The price mechanism, other things equal, will signal to entrepreneurs the shortage or surplus and this will damp down and eliminate the destabilising influences. The simple accelerator model is arithmetically sound but economically defective.

But can cycles be caused by powerful trades unions or by oil price rises by the OPEC nations?

---

5. Sir Dennis Robertson,'Mr Keynes and the rate of interest' in *Readings in the Theory of Income Distribution*, Philadelphia 1946, p. 440.

NEITHER UNIONS NOR IMPORTS

Consider the quantity theory $M_s V = PQ$ or $Q = M_s V/P$. Now assume a strong trade union negotiates an exceptionally high wage increase, well above any increase in productivity. For simplicity, assume productivity is unchanged. Then for the original level of wages and prices the equation can be written $Q_1 = M_s V/P_1$. This merely implies that price and quantity are inversely related as for any demand curve, individual or aggregate. If the average money price level now rises to P_2 because of the wage increase and because, possibly, the extra labour costs are passed on to the consumers, and if M_s and V are unchanged, then Q_1 must move down (say to Q_2) in the basic equation.

If Q_2, i.e. real goods and services produced and bought, falls, inventories accumulate, production is cut back and labour is laid off. The result of P_1 moving up to P_2 is unsold goods and abnormal unemployment. If the average price level continues at P_2, the unemployment will persist. If producers reduce their prices to sell off the unsold inventories, workers will have to lower the money wages they insist on getting for producers to be willing to hire them to replenish inventories.

Cost-push by trade unions, *per se*, cannot sustain an increase of the average money price level. If government does nothing, the abnormal unemployment will continue until the average price level and money wages decline. On the other hand, if government intervenes it will pursue an expansionary money policy, raising M_s, and/or an expansionary pure fiscal policy, raising V. Either way $M_s V$ will be larger and the P values which previously related to specific Q values will be higher at each and every output level (since $Q = M_s V/P$ and Q and $M_s V$ are numerators on their respective sides of the equation). Effectively, the community's demand curve has been moved up and to the right (or, in the Keynesian cross diagram, the $C + I + G$ line has moved up). Because of the active monetary or fiscal policies of government the cost-push of the trade unions and its immediate impact on the average price level, a higher P, has been ratified. There need not then be unsold inventories or abnormal unemployment tending to reduce this higher average money price. Given the new higher value of $M_s V$, there will be sufficient money expenditures to maintain total real output at the original Q level. Inflation, however, *will* have occurred, but only because government permitted it.

In a similar manner, a rise in import costs (even a substantial one like the oil price rises in 1973–4 or in 1978) cannot, unless ratified by government, result in sustained increase in the average money price level. As long as M_s and V remain constant the initial increase in the cost of imported goods would result in unsold goods and unemployment. This would persist until the *average* money price level fell to its original level. At that point, some money prices would be higher (e.g. those of oil or oil-related products) than originally and others would be lower. *Relative* prices would have changed, and so would *relative* quantities consumed, but there would have been no inflation.

A STAGFLATION MODEL

If $M_s V = PQ$ in period (1), and in period (2) the same equation holds (as it must, although with potentially different values for each of the four components), then $\Delta M_s.\Delta V = \Delta P.\Delta Q$ and (in percentage terms):[6]

$$\Delta M_s / M_s + \Delta V / V = \Delta P / P + \Delta Q / Q$$

which implies that the sum of money supply growth rate and

---

6. This is proved thus:

$$M^{\Delta M} V^{\Delta V} = P^{\Delta P} Q^{\Delta Q}$$

where the indices are the respective rates of change in the variables. Thus

$$\Delta M. \log M + \Delta V \log V = \Delta P \log P + \Delta Q \log Q$$

Differentiating throughout

$$\frac{\Delta M}{M} + \frac{\Delta V}{V} = \frac{\Delta P}{P} + \frac{\Delta Q}{Q}$$

the rate of change of velocity (which equals the percentage rate of change of $M_s V$) equals the sum of the inflation rate and the real output growth rate (which equals the percentage rate of change of PQ).

The equation can be rewritten:

$$\Delta P/P = (\Delta M_s/M_s + \Delta V/V) - \Delta Q/Q$$

which states that the inflation rate equals the rate of growth of total spending minus the real output growth rate.

Thus given a fixed level of spending growth, S_1, if real output growth were zero, inflation would be A per cent (figure 10.1). If, on the other hand, real output growth were A' per cent, inflation would be zero. All combinations for inflation between zero and A per cent can then be plotted as the line S_1, AA'. A lower rate of spending growth (say 5%) would be exemplified by a line such as BB'. That line shows all possible combinations of inflation and real output growth when total spending growth has fallen to 5%. The total spending growth line will rise (or fall) if $\Delta M_s/M_s$ or $\Delta V/V$ rises or falls. A reduction in $\Delta M_s/M_s$ could therefore, cause the total spending growth line to shift to the left.

If the economy always operated at capacity the real output growth rate would equal the capacity growth rate (as determined by shifts outwards in the production possibility frontier). But if the economy suffers from high inflation rates for prolonged periods it may lose the ability to grow. Since inflation raises real taxes, fewer and fewer resources will remain available for private sector productive investment or jobs.[7] More resources will be used on red tape, supersonic airliners, building grandiose universities and the like. The underlying

---

7. In fact so long as the resources are not diverted from the market sector (i.e. where goods are bought and sold) it does not matter, in principle, if the nationalised industries or private industries retain the resources. However, in practice, in Britain, it *does* matter since most nationalised industries are consistently running at real losses and so, along with non-market services such as the fire service, social workers, etc, they are supported by the private sector. 'The true deficits of the public corporations', Walter Eltis, *Lloyds Bank Review* 1979.

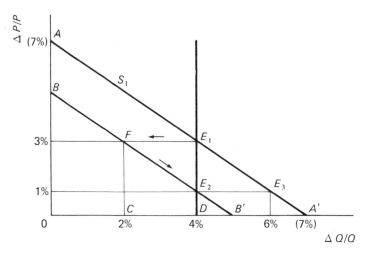

Figure 10.1

support of the private sector will get progressively weaker. With fewer new jobs created and a given rate of total spending growth, inflation will get worse and unemployment increase. The economy will 'stagflate' and move up the spending growth line.

Even if such long-run consequences are ignored, stagflation must emerge if changeable government policies are routinely implemented. Assume a fixed rate of capacity growth of 6%, and a total spending growth rate of S_1 (figure 10.1). E_3 is 'inflationary equilibrium'. Real output growth rate is the same as the capacity growth rate. Even though inflation is 1%, there is no recession. If, however, the economy is at E_1, given our previous assumption, there is now a 3% inflation rate, but only a 4% output growth rate, 2% less than the capacity growth rate of 6%. The economy is in a state of inflationary recession.

Consider again figure 10.1. The initial total spending growth rate is S_1 ($\Delta M/M + \Delta V/V$). Capacity growth is 4% and the economy is at a point of inflationary equilibrium E_1. If the Bank of England now reduces the money supply growth rate so that AA' falls to BB', the new inflationary equilibrium (E_2) sees the output growth rate unchanged and inflation reduced to 1%. But inflation will not immediately fall from 3% to 1%.

It will continue temporarily at 3% as though nothing had happened. Given BB', the real growth rate will therefore fall to 2% (point F) and the economy will continue to suffer in this way from stagflation until inflation begins to subside.

> On the average ... the total delay between a change in monetary growth and a change in the rate of inflation (takes) something like 12–18 months ... it is a long row to hoe to stop inflation that has been allowed to start. It cannot be stopped overnight.[8]

Why does it take so long (longer when the inflation rate is higher) to move from F to E_2? The reason is the familiar Keynesian observation that prices are not the first economic variable to adjust. Until each seller realises that inflation rate has definitely fallen *on average*, he will believe that he is only observing a transient downward movement around an existing, static mean. This *perceptions lag* must be overcome before sellers will reduce their prices. In the interim they will merely let inventories take the strain. Once the sellers realise that inflation has indeed fallen, that the demand fall for their product is permanent due to their maintaining a high price, there will be a *price search lag*. This occurs while sellers attempt to decide what the optimal new price level should be (a problem for microeconomics). Again, *contract lags* will inhibit price changes in some areas until legal contracts either expire or are renegotiated at new prices.

Finally, what is the government doing meantime, and where? It initiated the move from E_1 to F in order to reach E_2. This involves passing through the unemployment position of C. Electorally this will be unattractive. Expansionary fiscal and/ or monetary policies may be employed. If so, BB' will move out to the right and some position above E_2, perhaps even above E_1, would be arrived at. This is a much more likely outcome than persistently pushing the spending-growth line downward until it passes through point D with zero inflation. In the final analysis, government, and only government, is the cause of inflation.

---

8. Milton Friedman, *The Counter-Revolution in Monetary Theory*, Institute of Economic Affairs 1970, p. 23.

11
International Trade

Trade between nations is identical in principle to trade between persons. Both parties are made better off. To the simple analysis, however, must be added the dimension of money. Foreign sellers do not want sterling in exchange for goods, they want their own national currency. Similarly, British buyers want to pay in sterling and British sellers want sterling in return for goods. This is why there is a balance of payments account. On other occasions a foreign currency may be used by both traders, for example 'Euro-dollars'. What are these, and what if any, is the role of gold? What are tariffs and quotas? These and other related problems are now discussed.

THE PRINCIPLES OF FOREIGN TRADE

Assume two countries, Britain and Japan, have (for simplicity) straight line production possibility frontiers as in figure 11.1. They can trade only with each other or not at all. Any trading is done on a barter basis — money does not complicate the issue. The two countries can produce only two goods, cars and whisky, and Japan can produce more of either good than Britain (3 units of whisky or 6 units of cars, while Britain can only produce 2 units of whisky or 1 unit of cars: where 'units'

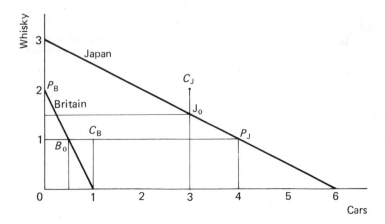

Figure 11.1

can represent millions of items or cases or whatever). Japan
has an absolute advantage over Britain in both goods (its
production possibility line lies further out to the right from
the origin).

Why then should the countries trade? Because Britain has
a *comparative* advantage over Japan in whisky. To produce 1
extra whisky unit in Britain costs the nation only 0.5 of a car
unit. In Japan the opportunity cost would be 2 car units.
Japan, on the other hand, has a comparative (and an absolute)
advantage over Britain in car production. The marginal cost
of 1 car in Japan is 0.5 whisky units. In Britain, if 1 extra
car unit was produced, 2 units of whisky would have to be
forgone.

If the two countries were at B_0 and J_0 respectively, then
consumption in each would be:

> Britain: B_0 consumption   1.0 whisky units
>   0.5 car units

> Japan: J_0 consumption   1.5 whisky units
>   3.0 car units.

Japan is better off than Britain in terms of what it can
produce and consume as a 'closed' economy, i.e. an economy
with no foreign trade. Now if each country *specialises* in the

goods in which it has a comparative advantage they can move (still without trade) to (say) P_B and P_J thus:

> Britain: P_B production   2 whisky units
>   0 cars
>
> Japan: P_J production   4 car units
>   1 whisky unit

If we now permit the countries to *trade* they can move to C_B and C_J respectively.

> Britain: C_B consumption   1 whisky unit
>   (1 to Japan)
>   1 car unit (1 from Japan)
>
> Japan: C_J consumption   3 car units (1 to Britain)
>   2 whisky units
>   (1 from Britain)

Both countries are made better off than they possibly could have been in the absence of trade. They have moved outwards to the right from their production possibility frontier. Each is consuming more than it could produce in isolation in the absence of trade.

DEMAND AND SUPPLY IN THE MARKET FOR INTERNATIONALLY TRADED GOODS

Figure 11.2 shows how (in the absence of transport costs) the world price for cars and whisky is determined. We will continue to assume a two-commodity, two-nation world. Figure 11.2(a) is the British domestic demand and supply situation for whisky. At any price above £3 per unit the quantity supplied would exceed that demanded. Thus at £3.50 the excess would equal *cd* units, at £4.00 *ab* units and so on. Figure 11.2(b) derives Britain's export supply curve from this apparatus. British whisky manufacturers, if offered £3 per

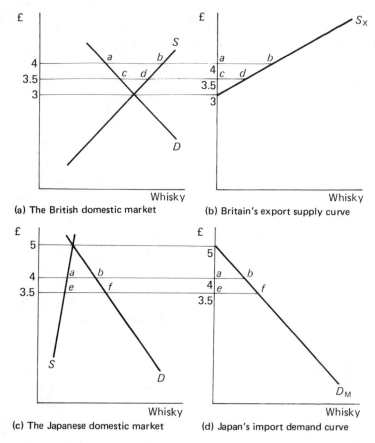

(a) The British domestic market

(b) Britain's export supply curve

(c) The Japanese domestic market

(d) Japan's import demand curve

Figure 11.2

unit would sell all they would willingly supply in Britain. But if they were offered £4 per unit they would produce *b* units, of which only *a* units would be taken up in the domestic market; *ab* units would therefore be exported.

Similarly, in Japan, figure 11.2(c) shows the domestic demand and supply curves for whisky. This time they are in equilibrium at £5.00 per unit. Should the domestic price be £4.00 the quantity demanded would expand to *b* units but suppliers would be less willing to manufacture whisky and would only produce *a* units. A shortage would arise. If trade was permitted Japanese consumers would buy none from overseas at £5.00 per unit, but *ab* units at £4.00, and still

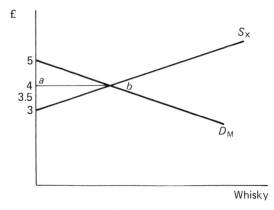

Figure 11.3 The international market

more, *ef* units at £3.50. Japan's import demand curve can thus
be derived, as in figure 11.2(d). An identical exercise could
be carried out for cars.

If figures 11.2(b) and 11.2(d) are now superimposed we
have the supply and demand for whisky in the international
market. The price settles at £4.00 per unit and *ab* units are
imported into Japan and exported from Britain (figure 11.3).
The market price of whisky in both countries is, of course,
determined by the price in the international market. Thus in
Britain the price rises to £4.00 and in Japan it falls. Whisky
consumption falls to *a* units in Britain, and rises to *b* units
in Japan (on figures 11.2(a) and (c) respectively). The British
pay more for their whisky and the Japanese less.

The situation would be reversed in the car market. The
British would pay less and the Japanese more.

QUOTAS AND TARIFFS

Although both Britain and Japan have benefited from trade
as total nations or populations, four groups of people are
superficially and in the short run worse off. (The total nation
in each case has moved out from its production possibility
frontier.) Japanese consumers are now paying higher prices
for their cars, as are British consumers for their whisky (£4

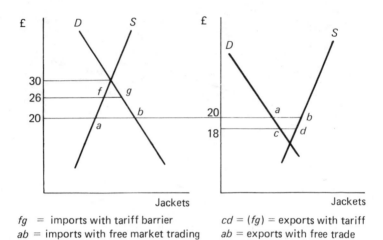

fg = imports with tariff barrier   cd = (fg) = exports with tariff
ab = imports with free market trading   ab = exports with free trade

(a) The British domestic market   (b) The Hong Kong domestic market

Figure 11.4

instead of £3 per whisky unit). Similarly, British car producers (managers, workers and providers of capital) are now manufacturing fewer cars than before. In Japan the situation in the whisky industry is also troubled. Output has fallen from the old equilibrium level, at £5 per unit in figure 11.2(c) to point *e* on that diagram, even though consumption has risen to point *f*.

Thus foreign trade can often appear to be unattractive to special interest groups and it is common to hear industrialists, trade unionists and others calling for the 'protection' of tariffs or quotas. Tariffs and quotas, of course, are merely devices to force consumers to consume goods which they value less rather than goods which they value more. This can be illustrated by an example. Consider a situation where British textile manufacturers or unions persuade the government to impose an £8 tariff on Hong Kong sports jackets. If no tariff existed these jackets would sell on the world market (and so the British market) at £20 each. Figure 11.4 shows how the imposition of the tariff forces Britons to pay a higher price for the jackets. (At first the price rises to £28, of which £8 goes to the government.) Their valuation of sports jackets will not change, so their demand curve will remain unaltered.

But given a higher price the British will travel up their demand curve, so buying fewer jackets.

But if fewer jackets are sold, the price the Hong Kong manufacturers will find it profitable to charge will fall. They will move down their (unchanged) supply curve in figure 11.4(b) to (say) d. This represents either or both of a contraction in output by existing Hong Kong firms or a reduction in their number. It is on the price level associated with d (£18) that the £8 tariff will ultimately be levied. Thus the price eventually paid by British buyers will be £26.

The tariff burden is partly borne by the British consumer and partly by the Hong Kong manufacturer. British manufacturers, however, are better off since their selling price is now £26, not £20, and more people are employed making jackets in Britain.

Quotas are identical in effect. Hong Kong will only sell cd units to Britain (if fg is the quota) at a price of £26. Hong Kong's supply curve is raised up and to the left as manufacturers find that their costs are raised at each and every output level. The cost rise may be due to the need to bid for import licenses from the British government, or to the need to engage in more or less morally desirable forms of persuasion to encourage British bureaucrats to issue licences to particular Hong Kong exporters.

THE BALANCE OF PAYMENTS

Exporters only wish to be paid in the currency of their own country. Yen have no value to a Briton, but he could not buy Japanese cars without them. Yet importers are only interested in paying in their own currency.

The balance of payments accounts of a country keep track of the supply and demand for pounds on the foreign exchange market. The supply represents payments by British people to foreigners. The demand for pounds is made by people who wish to make payments into Britain.

Table 11.1 gives an example of the British balance of payments. There are two basic accounts: 'current account' and

Table 11.1 UK Balance of Payments, 1976 (£ million)

		Receipts from foreigners	Payments to foreigners
Current account			
Visible trade — Exports		25,416	
Imports			28,987
Visible balance	(−3571)		
Invisibles			
Services, profits and dividends (net)		4,364	
Government			2,198
Invisible balance	(+2166)		
Current balance	(−1405)		
Investment and other capital transactions			
Investment in UK private sector		2,051	
UK private investment overseas			2,100
Other capital outflows from the public or private sectors			2,174
Balance for official financing (−3628) (Current balance plus investment and capital balance)			
Official Financing			
Liabilities to foreign agencies by government or public sector		1,791	
IMF accounts		1,018	
Additions to or subtractions from official reserves		853	
Other			34
Total official financing	(+3628)	35,493	35,493

'investment and other capital transactions'. The current account shows receipts or payments from exports and imports, both goods and services ('invisibles' such as insurance, shipping, tourism and investment income from or to multinational firms). In the table there is a negative figure on the so-called 'balance of trade', not entirely compensated for by a positive figure for invisibles. There was a deficit on current account. This, although often bewailed by the media and by parliamentarians is largely irrelevant. A deficit or surplus is not good or bad in itself. The gains from trade are not a positive balance of trade (which is merely a book-keeping balancing item) but rather that we move off our production possibility frontier. We pay less in terms of real goods forgone if we import than we would have to if we made them ourselves.

'Investment and other capital transactions' include private and government investment in Britain or overseas. Short term inflows and outflows in this section of the accounts can be very sensitive to variations in international interest or exchange rates.

'Official financing' is that part of the balance of payments accounts which is necessary to keep the receipts and payments columns equal. If, for example, we export more than we import, receipts from foreigners would exceed payments to foreigners. Official financing would then be negative. The Bank of England would receive gold, foreign currencies or foreign government bonds for which it would pay sterling, or alternatively outstanding debt to the International Monetary Fund might be paid off. The reverse would occur if (as in table 11.1) there was a negative balance of payments figure (in this case a deficit of £3628 million).

The operation may be explained by illustration. When a foreigner receives a pound he sells it to a foreign exchange dealer for his own currency. The various dealers then sell pounds to other buyers for other currencies, depending on their clients' needs. One such buyer could be a Central Bank. For example, if the Federal Reserve Bank of the USA sees that so many pounds are being sold that the pound price of the dollar is rising, it may step in and buy pounds with dollars so pushing the dollar price in pounds back down (and the pound price in dollars back up).

The Federal Reserve may keep the pounds or deposit them at the Bank of England, or buy British government bonds (so possibly affecting our money supply). In any event Britain incurs a liability to the Federal Reserve. Such liabilities form the largest part of Official Financing in table 11.1.

If the excess supply of pounds is not purchased by foreigners when we buy more abroad than we sell then either the value of the pound falls, or the pounds must be bought with gold or foreign exchange reserves or borrowing from the IMF[1] must occur.

THE FOREIGN EXCHANGE VALUE OF THE POUND

The Federal Reserve's hypothetical purchases of pounds in our last illustration was not the result of any thoughtless altruism towards sterling. If the pound is one of the main assets of the Federal Reserve (as table 11.1 suggests it is) then it is in the interest of the Federal Reserve to keep the price of the pound up in terms of dollars. Moreover, the Federal Reserve may be under pressure from the US government to aid American exporting firms and help American domestic firms to ward off imports. One way to do this (in addition to tariffs or quotas) is to push down the price of the dollar in terms of other currencies like the pound. The same argument, of course, would hold in reverse for the Bank of England.

So far we have generally assumed fixed and known exchange rates between pounds and other currencies. This need not be the case. Exchange rates can be fixed, they can fluctuate freely according to supply and demand, and so currencies can be treated like any other commodity with a futures market, or they can move in a semi-controlled fashion as most do at present. ('Dirty-floating' is the phrase used for this half-way house.)

To illustrate, assume two countries and two commodities. Britain and Holland trade whisky and Dutch bulbs. Assume there is a rate of exchange of £1 for 5 guilders. Figure 11.5 shows the export supply and import demand curves for the respective countries. Whisky sells at £4 per bottle. Holland buys 50 million bottles and therefore demands £200 million from the foreign exchange market. This is point a in figure 11.6. If the pound's value now falls for some reason to 4 guilders D_1 will move to D_2 in figure 11.5(a). The Dutch

---

1. The IMF was set up in 1944. All countries deposited 'quotas' in it of which only one quarter needed to be in gold. The remainder could be in their own currencies. They were then entitled to borrow from the IMF for credits or foreign currencies.

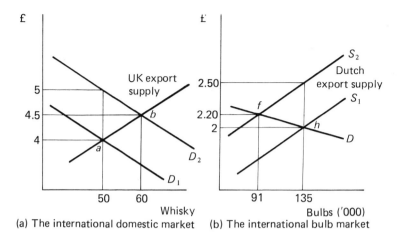

(a) The international domestic market (b) The international bulb market

Figure 11.5

would and did pay 20 guilders per bottle. They still will, but the demand curves are drawn in sterling values. 20 guilders now equal £5, not £4. This results in a new equilibrium whisky price of £4.50 in the international market and 60 million bottles are sold. (The supply prices of British distillers are unchanged.)

The Dutch now demand (60 million × £4.50) £270 million on the foreign exchange market (i.e. point *b* in figure 11.6).

Turning now to the bulb market, S_1 is Holland's export supply at the original exchange rate. This results in a selling price of £2 per thousand bulbs and 135,000 bulbs sold. Britain buys these bulbs and supplies £270 million to the foreign exchange market to obtain the necessary guilders with which to pay for them (point *h* in figure 11.6). When the pound's price falls to 4 guilders, the Dutch farmers are unperturbed. They will continue supplying the same quantity of bulbs for any given guilder price as before. But figure 11.5(b) is drawn on a sterling basis; that is, the sterling supply curve must fall to the left, to S_2, if at each and every sterling price the same guilders income is to be realised. Farmers had been receiving £270 million (i.e. 1350 million guilders). To continue receiving 1350 million guilders they would need a new sterling price of £2.50 (4 × 2.50 × 135 = 1350),

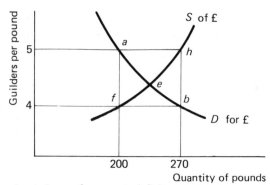

ab = balance of payments deficit
fb = surplus (from Britain's viewpoint)

Figure 11.6

albeit with an unchanged guilder price. In fact the new equilibrium price is £2.20, the quantity of bulbs sold is 91,000 and the supply of pounds to the foreign exchange market falls to £200 million, point *f* in figures 11.5 and 11.6. (91,000 X 2.2 = 200 million approximately).

This example shows how exports (imports) can be encouraged (discouraged) by the Bank of England if it induces an exchange rate fall, and vice versa. That was the reasoning behind the devaluation of 1967. It also illustrates, however, that in a free foreign exchange market the value of the pound would settle at *e* in figure 11.6. Payments to and from foreigners would exactly balance, there would be no need for official financing in the balance of payments accounts and there would be no need for an IMF to lend to countries persistently in deficit.

EURODOLLARS[2]

(This section can be omitted on brief courses.)

Eurodollars, or more accurately 'Eurocurrencies' since dollars are now only around 70% of the total, are deposited with banks located outside the countries by which they are issued. A Eurodollar deposit resulting from the dollar

2. See Paul Bareau, 'The international money and capital markets' in *City Lights*, Institute of Economic Affairs 1979.

proceeds of an export by country A to the USA but invested in a bank in country B has an offsetting balance in the necessary deposit made by the bank from B in an American bank. The Eurodeposit can, in the normal course of fractional reserve banking, then be used to increase the money supply of country B. The impact need not, of course, be limited to B but can extend to C, D or E or wherever the increase in deposits based on the original Eurodollar are redeposited outside America.

Whether for good or ill, Eurocurrencies arose from government legislation. Regulation Q in America limited the amount of interest American banks could pay to depositors, thus discouraging dollar deposits in the USA. In Europe many countries, at least until recently, had controls governing the volume of currency citizens could take out of their country. Dollars were thus at one and the same time discouraged (by limited interest rates) from remaining in the USA and encouraged (by legal restrictions on international movements of currencies within Europe) to cross the Atlantic where they could meet a demand for liquidity which Europeans had but could not fulfil outside of their own particular national boundaries.

THE ROLE OF GOLD

If success is to be measured by the yardstick of relatively stable average prices then a gold or metallic standard wins hands down over the fiat money system of the last five decades. Why have governments gone off the 'gold standard' and what is meant by the phrase?

The classical gold standard ruled from 1815–1914. This meant that exchange rates were fixed, not by arbitrary government control, but because the pound, dollar, mark, franc and so on were tied to a specified weight of gold. In effect this meant that the world had a single medium of money with all of the advantages that entailed.

Why did the system break down? First, governments monopolised the processes of minting and note issue. This

was apparently harmless until the catastrophe of World War
1 encouraged governments to inflate their supply of fiat
and paper money and so made it impossible for themselves
to keep their pledges of redeemability[3] which were generally
printed on their currencies. Most countries then went off the
gold standard (except the USA) and most currencies were
allowed to float to a greater or lesser degree against each other.
All fell in value in relation to both gold and the dollar.

Britain entered World War 1 with the pound equal to $4.86
(in gold equivalent) but by the end of the war the inflation
generated by printing money had reduced the pound's value
to $3.50. Had Britain revalued the pound in relation to gold
at that price, all might have been well. However, Britain
combined wartime inflation with an attempt (in 1926) to
return to gold at $4.86 to the £1. To succeed in doing this
the UK would have had to deflate its money supply severely
and lower prices in its vital export markets. In fact Britain
continued to inflate, real wage rates rose, thus compounding
the problem and throughout the 1920s Britain experienced
high unemployment and depressed exports when most of the
world was experiencing an economic boom.

When America entered its depression in 1929, due to
what Friedman[4] had called a 'mistaken' cut in the money
supply by the Federal Reserve Bank, Britain was pulled
further into the abyss as each nation adopted self-defeating
self-sufficiency programmes of tariffs and quotas which
merely resulted in sharply declining world trade and a beggar-
my-neighbour situation. A 'gold-exchange' standard was
entered into. America remained on gold, redeeming dollars
on demand. The UK, however, only redeemed in large bars,
not in coin, suitable only for international transactions.
Furthermore, Britain redeemed debts in dollars also, while
other nations paid off their obligations in either of the two
'reserve' currencies, dollars or sterling.

---

3. For example, the written 'promise' on a Bank of England £1 note is
   meaningless. A gold sovereign cannot be obtained in exchange for it.
4. Between 1929 and 1933 the US money supply was cut by one third.
   Milton Friedman, *The Counter Revolution in Monetary Theory*, IEA
   Occasional Paper No. 33, 1970, p. 16.

Now (the late 1920s) when the UK inflated its money supply and experienced a deficit on its balance of payments, the mechanism did *not* work quickly to restrict inflation. For, instead of other countries redeeming their pounds for gold, so deflating the British money supply back to its original level (and thus influencing downward pressure on British prices both in home and export markets), many kept their pounds and expanded their own currencies on top of them.[5] Nevertheless, the UK tended still to lose gold. Instead of repealing unemployment insurance provisions, contracting credit or going back to a more realistic gold parity, Britain turned to the USA for help. For if America expanded its supply of dollars she need no longer demand gold from Britain to make up any deficiency in Britain's payments balance. 'In short the American public was nominated to suffer the burdens of inflation and subsequent collapse in order to maintain the British government and the British trade union movement in the style to which they insisted on becoming accustomed.'[6] The Federal Reserve System's aid to the UK from 1924 to 1928 is well documented. The subsequent money supply cut blamed by Friedman for the depression was simply the natural outcome of the artificially generated money supply increase of the 1920s. Government-induced slump followed government-generated boom as night followed day. In 1931 when France attempted to cash in its sterling balances for gold at the Bank of England the system collapsed and Britain went completely off the gold standard.

In the USA the gold standard was abandoned in 1933–34, but in 1934 it did return to an unusual form of standard in which the dollar was redefined as 1/35th of an ounce of gold and was redeemable only to foreign governments and central banks.

In 1944 the Bretton Woods Agreement (at which the IMF was created) took the world back to the gold exchange standard of the 1920s. This time only the dollar was redeemable, not the pound as well. Each currency was pegged at a

5. There is a parallel here with the Eurocurrencies of the 1970s.
6. Rothbard, *op. cit.*, pp. 131–2.

fixed rate of exchange[7] to the dollar, to be altered only if a nation had a persistent imbalance on its balance of payments accounts. The system worked better than the short-sighted, trade-restrictionist 1930s, but like the 1920s it lived on borrowed time. The USA ended World War 2 with a huge stock of gold. A 'dollar shortage' existed and American foreign aid was used by other countries to import from America. Again, as in the 1920s, the dollar had been valued against other countries' currencies at their pre-war levels. It was consequently undervalued, making American goods appear 'cheap' and other countries' goods 'dear' on world markets. Countries which expanded their money supply and ran balance of payments deficits soon had to devalue (e.g. Britain in 1949 to $2.80 and in 1967 to $2.40) in the absence of classical gold standard discipline. Meanwhile countries which pursued courses of stricter monetary self-discipline grew restless at having to hold a reserve currency (viz. dollars) which was becoming increasingly overvalued instead of under-valued. (America had been pursuing expansionist monetary policies to finance social welfare programmes in the Kennedy-Johnson years. This inflationary policy was compounded by the Vietnam war and the US government deficits which that caused.) The American average price level was rising, so dollars held abroad were falling in real value. However dollars remained redeemable only at 1/35th ounce of gold and so countries which had pursued less inflationist policies, such as Japan, West Germany and France, began to get rid of their unwanted dollars by redeeming them in America. The French, in particular, did not approve of the Americans obtaining goods on world markets by the device of printing dollars of ever-diminishing value. America's trade deficit (i.e. its excess of consumption over production) was thus being financed by surpluses on the balance of payments accounts of other countries (i.e. they experienced a deficiency of consumption of real good *vis à vis* their production). As the American gold stock dwindled (by over one half) the Bretton

---

7. Or moveable only by one per cent of their adopted values.

Woods Agreement had to break down and did so in 1968. A 'two-tier' gold market was then established. Governments and central banks continued to trade gold at $35 per ounce, but in the outside world the free market price was allowed to rise or fall according to forces of supply and demand. The difference between the two prices (around $100 per ounce) ensured that this temporary patch-up would not survive. (The temptation to redeem 35 dollars for one ounce of gold in Washington and then resell the metal elsewhere for $100 more was too obvious to ignore.) In 1971 Bretton Woods was totally abandoned and the dollar became a completely fiat currency for the first time in its history. In 1972 the major trading countries tried to establish a system of fixed exchange rates unlinked to gold in any way.

This collapsed in turn in 1973 as different countries pursued policies resulting in differing real values for their currencies. Floating currencies or managed ('dirty') floats have been the norm since 1973 (a managed float being one where the relevant central bank attempts to keep its currency at or near a chosen price in the foreign exchange market by buying or selling foreign exchange).

The 'dirtier' the float, the sooner will it collapse (history and theory have illustrated this to us). As we have seen, freely floating exchange rates eliminate balance of payments deficits or surpluses (except between arbitrarily chosen opening and closing accounting dates). Gold, however, remains the one medium which, *purely because of its limited supply, not because of any mystical properties,* can provide the advantage of fixed exchange rates (future certainty regarding the prices of foreign goods) without their disadvantages (government interference with international trade and the losses which arise from aborted or hampered trade). And it does this while simultaneously providing the invaluable benefit of discipline over government in its management of the economy. Money supply expansion cannot be pursued for long. If it is, domestic prices will rise, exports become uncompetitive, imports cheap, and gold will flow out of the country. The process will continue until the government can no longer sell its bonds to pay for its profligacy but must instead contract its expenditure and the money supply. When this occurs price levels will fall and international equilibrium be reattained.[8]

The alternative, when no independent check is placed on government, is inflation followed by price and wage controls, followed by social discontent at resulting price and wage disparities and at taxation levels. It remains to be seen whether or not this progression need follow either of its two logical courses: (a) to a wholly *dirigiste* economy where individual freedom of contract is wiped out and private property and choice effectively cease or (b) to social upheaval of the most unpleasant sort. Alternatively, can an economic and social about-turn be accomplished? Can governments be leashed, by a return to the classical gold standard or some other equally effective mechanism? Monetarists argue that a slowly expanding money supply, allowed to grow within the limits of GNP or some other given variable, would provide the necessary discipline over government. Gold standard advocates agree in broad principle with the objectives of the monetarists, but doubt that government would so discipline itself with a policy tool over which it itself has control. Both agree that discretionary upswings and downswings in the supply of money can increase government popularity in the short run but produce destabilisation and depression or inflation in the longer term.

Gold, however, is far from being universally reaccepted. In 1970 the IMF introduced Special Drawing Rights (SDRs). These are nick-named 'paper-gold' and can be exchanged by member nations in the same way as ordinary foreign currencies or gold. They are valued by using some weighted average of the world's major currencies. This paper reserve designed to replace gold was originally supported strongly by Britain and the USA. The 'hard money' countries of Western Europe

---

8. The advantages of gold, then, are mainly 'negative'. Uncertainty about future foreign prices can be overcome in the 'futures' market for currencies. The other and main benefit of gold, the curbing of government power, cannot be obtained so easily. Its disadvantages, if that is what they are, are the music-hall joke of digging it out of one hole in the Transvaal to bury it in another in Threadneedle Street.

strongly opposed their establishment, fearing (in retrospect, correctly) that governments would then be able to inflate their money supply, checked only by the willingness of the IMF as banker to allow persistent borrowing. The double digit inflation achieved by the US and UK in 1979 but avoided by other countries seems to lend support to this view. Gold, meanwhile, has risen in price to over $400 per ounce, or, more accurately, the price of the dollar has fallen from 1/35th of an ounce of gold to nearly 1/400th of an ounce. Most American and British economics texts continue to advocate the demonetisation of gold as a foreign currency reserve. At this juncture the advice is both appealing and attractive. It is appealing in as much as it would remove the final restraint from government inflationary tendencies. It is attractive in so far as central banks with gold can and do now revalue their foreign currency reserves every time gold rises in (free market) price.

Free economies have not existed long enough for us to be able to predict which outcome is the likelier, nor, if the optimistic result occurs, which policy tool (a classical gold standard or non-discretionary monetarism) will be the better to stave off further problems. All we can assert is the proven efficacy of the classical gold standard in a century of practice.

CONCLUDING THOUGHTS

If we recall our definition of GNP (page 15) we can see that algebraically it cannot be restricted to the simplistic $C + I + G$ equation. But it must be rewritten as

$$\text{GNP} = C + I + G + X - M = PQ = M_s V$$
where $M =$ imports
$X =$ exports.

Obviously $M_s V$, the money supply times its velocity, is also affected by international trade and not unaffected, as assumed in earlier chapters. A rise in exports results in sterling being deposited in the exporter's British bank account (and so M_s

and the price of the pound may rise) and vice versa for imports. [The actual mechanics are that the exporter receives foreign currency. His bank surrenders this currency to the Bank of England for sterling. This increases the exporter's deposit at his own bank. It also increases the bank's deposit at the Bank of England. The Bank places the currency in the official reserves held in the Exchange Equalisation Account. The Bank could, if it so wished, then sell bills equal in value to the increase in bank reserves to prevent either a single or multiple M_s expansion. This is easier to say than to do, however. First, there are millions of export transactions. Second, the process is operating in reverse for importers, thus complicating the issue still further. Third, if the transaction is conducted initially in sterling, the process will occur abroad outside the Bank's immediate control or ken. It will only show up as the British commercial bank's deposits increase for some (to the Bank) unknown reason. Finally, the Bank may or may not be attempting to manage the exchange rate as well as the money supply; in which case, say it wished to let the exchange rate move down, it would not buy the foreign currency and place it in the official reserves because that would keep the pound's price up. Rather, the foreign exchange market would be allowed to absorb the currency.] In like manner bond sales to foreigners for sterling (via the Bank of England) can provide government with the wherewithal to fund a deficit. Again M_s, the average price level and the price of the pound on the foreign exchange market may tend to rise as more pounds are demanded to put on deposit in Britain. If the average price level rises too far as a result of these movements British goods may become uncompetitive in world markets, unemployment may result in exporting industries and so the GNP may begin to decline. The scenario variations are endless.

12
Conclusions

This chapter summarises some of the foregoing. In addition it introduces some of the recent developments in modern macro-economics over which there is still much disagreement. The chapter ends with a brief recapitulation of recent economic history.

THE STANDARD FRAMEWORK AGAIN

The previous chapters have indicated that fiscal or monetary policies can be used to raise or lower aggregate demand. To the extent that the effects are not inflationary (i.e. it is real goods or services which increase in quantity, not their average price level) then real imports will rise (either as finished goods or as inputs for goods to be manufactured here). Thus such an expansionary policy can lower unemployment but affect the balance of payments by making imports larger relative to exports. This can be expressed diagramatically as:

expansion → a rise in domestic demand
→ an increase in employment
→ an increase in exports.

It has also been indicated that exchange rate policies (i.e. devaluations, revaluations or 'dirty' floats) can be used to encourage or discourage expenditure on domestic production

by altering the relative prices of domestic and overseas products. A devaluation, for instance, encourages foreign consumers to buy British; and it discourages imports, as foreign
goods are made more expensive in sterling terms. In consequence aggregate demand (within Britain) rises, unemployment falls and exports rise in relation to imports. (This is
provided that foreign and domestic consumers are sufficiently
price sensitive to change their volume of purchases to a degree
which will more than offset the relative price changes. This
need not be so. The other proviso is that net domestic savings
must rise since if more resources now go overseas in the shape
of exports less is available in this country to provide the
wherewithal for investment. These assumptions may be unrealistic.) Making these assumptions we can once again express
the situation diagramatically as:

> devaluation → export prices falling in terms of
> foreign currencies and import prices
> rising in terms of sterling
> → an export volume rise
> an import volume fall
> → a rise in aggregate demand
> → an increase in employment

Thus (given the assumptions) while both expansionary
policies and devaluation may lower employment, their impact
on the balance of payments is not the same. In the former it
can reduce a surplus or increase the need for official financing,
in the latter case it can increase a surplus or reduce the need
for official financing.

Figure 12.1 illustrates these two relationships. Devaluation
moves the economy upwards, expansion moves the economy
to the right. Consider the intersection of the axes as representing a 'desired' level of employment and a 'satisfactory' balance
of payments. This is the government's economic target. The
line AA' shows the combination of policies which would
leave aggregate demand $(C + I + G + X - M)$ unchanged. BB'
shows the combination of policies which would leave the
balance of payments unchanged. AA' and BB' slope in

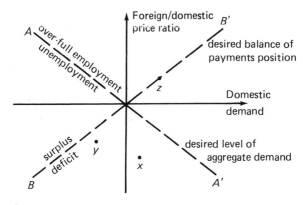

Figure 12.1

opposite directions since expansion and devaluation have opposite effects on the balance of payments.

In order to move to the origin from any point on the diagram both policies are required. For example at point x, with unemployment and a deficit, devaluation and contraction would be resorted to. At point y, again with unemployment and a deficit on balance of payments account, devaluation and expansion would be the prescribed policy mix.

Only with points on one or other axis would one policy alone suffice. If the economy lay on either AA' or BB', however, say z, with over-full employment and a satisfactory balance of payments then revaluation and contraction are required, but expenditure must be switched from domestic to overseas goods if the economy is not to move off BB'.

THE FULL MULTIPLIER

In Chapter 6 we assumed a closed economy where the Keynesian multiplier was defined algebraically as $1/(1 - \text{MPC})$. If we now try to make the model more complete and recall that national income (or expenditure) is given by

$$Y = C + I + G + X - M - T_{\text{I}}$$

where T_{I} is indirect taxation, and add that $C = \text{MPC}\,(Y - T_{\text{D}})$

where T_D is direct taxation, and given that total income is either paid in taxes, consumed or saved so that

$$Y = T_D + C + S$$

then $\quad C + I + G + X - M - T_I = T_D + C + S$

or $\quad I + G + X = S + T + M$

(where $T = T_I + T_D$). The left-hand side represents injections into aggregate demand, the right-hand side components are leakages. In Chapter 6 a rise in investment was multiplied up by $1/(1 - \text{MPC})$ (given autonomous investment), but here we have six components affecting any change in Y. Given (ignoring taxation for the moment) that all income is either spent or saved, then (in equilibrium)

$$I = S$$
$$= Y - \text{MPC}.Y$$

(it will be recalled that MPC is the slope of the consumption function). Also in equilibrium, injections equal leakages, so if we assume that both taxes and imports will rise with income we can write:

$$T_D = t_d Y$$

and $\quad M = m Y$

Now by substitution into the national income equation

$$Y = C + I + G + X - M - T_I$$

we obtain $\quad Y = \text{MPC} \, (Y - t_d \, Y) + I + G + X - mY$

and so
$$Y = \frac{I + G + X}{1 - \text{MPC}(1 - t_d) + m}$$

$$= (I + G + X)\left(\frac{1}{1 - \text{MPC}(1 - t_d) + m}\right)$$

which is the full multiplier relationship showing how each of the injections is multiplied up to obtain Y. The multiplier is higher, the higher is MPC and/or the lower are tax and import propensities.

This increased algebraic sophistication, however, in no way removes the economic doubts cast on the concept of the multiplier and the ability to abuse or misinterpret it which we discussed earlier.

FURTHER PROBLEMS

The values for the MPC, import, export, investment and tax payment propensities are of consequence for more than the multiplier alone. They also affect the relative slopes of the line AA' and BB' in figure 12.1. For example, in figure 12.2(a) and 12.2(b) the two lines are reproduced with differing relative slopes. If the economy is at the same starting point x, in 12.2(a) the dual prescription of expansion and devaluation can either take the economy progressively closer to the desired policy objective, 12.2(a), or even further away from it 12.2(b). But these diagrams assume that exchange rate policy is weaker than monetary or fiscal policy (the initial and stronger movement is to the right — on domestic demand). It may not be, in which case, the movement from x would tend predominantly upwards and clockwise. Thus figure 12.2(a) would then represent an economy becoming progressively destabilised, and 12.2(b) one moving towards equilibrium. Which of these four possibilities is more correct will probably vary situation by situation.

Thus because of the sheer complexity of the study of macroeconomics, one would imagine the student would be made humble and the economist a model of caution. We have seen that governments often know nothing of this humility or caution. There is, then, all the more reason under such circumstances for economists to recommend the adoption of consistently neutral rules and not discretionary action, the pursuit of modest goals and not grandiose schemes.

If this text has conveyed to businessmen and others

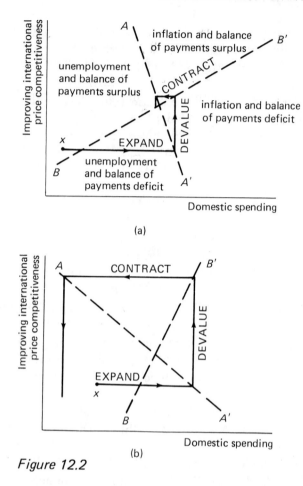

Figure 12.2

even the message contained in the last three sentences it will have achieved it purpose. If it can influence those who create or guide macroeconomic policies it will have accomplished even more. This statement is possibly best illustrated by the next few pages recapitulating the nature of the current economic dilema.

RECENT HISTORY AND PROBLEMS

The pattern of the 1950s and early 1960s is epitomised by the position of the USA. She promoted a general stabilisation of prices and liberalisation of international trade and took the lead in setting up a free market global economy. This changed, however, in the early and mid-1960s when America's commitment to monetary good management altered. Her monetary policy became increasingly expansionary due to efforts to achieve lower unemployment, fight a war and greatly increase spending on social welfare programmes. The latter objective was pursued equally or more vigorously in the UK.

Government expenditure as a share of GNP rose rapidly in most industrial countries. The wealth created by an efficient market economy created expectations of continuing progress. This led government to pander to pressure groups who wished to force the pace of growth. The money supply was further increased, and the end result was an inflationary boom followed by the cyclically inevitable slow-down in economic expansion itself. The process was almost universal but the sheer size of the US economy implied that the American monetary increase was communicated to the rest of the world by the system of fixed exchange rates. The culmination was the inflation of 1973–75.

This inflation partly *caused* the OPEC oil price rise. In real terms oil had been lagging far behind the prices of most OPEC imports from the oil-consuming countries. But the cause of the current slump was not the oil price rise but the monetary expansion of the late 1960s and early 1970s. It, in turn, was accompanied by government policies which exacerbate slump rather than ones which are neutral towards it. Income redistribution policies, anti-pollution laws and the like have all encouraged malinvestment and a reduction in returns to investment, i.e. profits. Not only are returns reduced but the incentives to work and to develop new skills have also fallen. A large part of the individual's income now takes the form of a 'social wage' rather than a reward for productive effort. Workers and firms have become increasingly shielded from competition. Investment returns from profitable opportunities (those that consumers will have a demand for) have declined; in consequence, so has investment in such areas and so economic growth has faltered.

On the demand side of the industrial economies governments have lost what, if any, power they had permanently to
influence the economy. Individuals now expect, and so discount, the kind of monetary policy shifts that in the past may
have been effective. People have adapted and learned over the
past decade. The three macro-markets, bonds, labour and
goods now form their expectations in new ways that are
damaging to the economy. Markets are anticipating the impact
of policy decisions on interest and exchange rates as, or
before, they are announced.

In the mid-1960s it was still possible to boost the economy
(even if with malinvestment) by a relatively small monetary
stimulus. Most people did not realise what was happening
when more money poured into the economy. Spending rose
and producers were misled into a belief that demand had
really risen and so hired more workers and increased production.

Time preferences, however, had not altered. Wages and
prices rose faster but the rises in demand proved to be temporary. As each dose of money supply increase wore off ever
larger stimuli were needed. Each recoil in output and employment resulted in the inflation ratchet rising by a further
notch.

As markets inevitably began to learn from years of this
experience and to foresee its consequences, the reaction lag
between money supply changes and inflation grew ever briefer.
And so the impact of the policies on the economy grew ever
smaller. By similar reasoning, the converse – that is, announced
monetary contraction followed by failure to stick to short run
unpleasant policies – has also been greeted by growing
incredulity. Thus money supply growth results in ever-rising
inflation rates while contraction is apparently futile.

The above scenario has fitted the history of the UK, Canada,
Italy and France for 1975–6. Since then all four have pro-
ceeded cautiously, neither daring to reflate nor deflate in any
overtly vigorous way. The USA in 1979 had reached the
situation of this national group. Although US monetary policy
has tightened, the Federal Reserve is aware, like its foreign

opposite numbers, that the short-term impact on inflation will be small but the political repercussions could be prompt.

Only Germany, Japan and Switzerland, with their traditional tight money policies, have avoided the negative implications of adaptive expectations as described above.

So the objective must be to restore the markets' confidence in the now generally stated and accepted government commitment to tight monetary control and low inflation rates. But this is not conceivable so long as each country is free to follow whatever monetary policy best suits its short-term political goals. External discipline, say by way of a metallic exchange standard, will be essential. One way to achieve this end is for the major nations to make a joint commitment to stabilise their currencies against each other's (e.g. as in the new European Monetary System) whereby each agrees to allow changes in its Central Bank's foreign assets to be fully reflected in their respective money supplies. 'Exporting' inflation and unemployment by successive devaluations would no longer be possible. Such an agreement would be the key to effective discipline. A country whose price level rose faster than those of others would have to intervene in the foreign exchange market to support its currency. The loss of reserves due to this intervention would put downward pressure on its rate of money growth and so bring its inflation rate back into line with the average of the group.

This sounds attractive but it is unlikely to work. It flies in the face of all past history, which predicts that governments do not lightly accept such external discipline. The optimistic forecaster can but hope for a return to the gold standard which worked so well until the global tragedy of 1914.

Statistical Appendix

	Money stock (M_3) (£m)	Velocity $(GNP \div M_3)$	Return on undated UK bonds (Consols)	Value of changes in inventories (£m)
1966	13555	2.2	—	342
1967	15000	2.1	6.69	336
1968	16092	2.1	7.39	460
1969	16596	2.2	8.88	446
1970	18175	2.2	9.16	444
1971	20541	2.2	9.05	110
1972	26245	1.8	9.11	62
1973	33478	1.7	10.85	1412
1974	37698	1.7	14.95	1138
1975	40573	2.0	14.66	—1423
1976	45124	2.1	14.25	359

	Unemployment rate expressed as per cent of total labour force	Public sector borrowing requirement (£m)	Wholesale prices index (manufactured goods) 1970 = 100	Bank rate (or minimum lending rate, 1971–76) (averages)
1966	1.5	961	—	7.0
1967	2.3	1863	—	6.75
1968	2.5	1279	89.9	7.6
1969	2.5	—466	93.4	8.0
1970	2.6	—17	100.0	7.35
1971	3.4	1373	109.0	5.5
1972	3.8	2047	114.8	7.0
1973	2.7	4168	123.2	10.5
1974	2.6	6336	152.0	11.5
1975	4.2	10515	188.7	11.0
1976	5.8	9512	219.6	12.0

	GNP less capital consumption, viz national income (£m)	GDP (at factor cost and constant price) 1970 = 100	Current balance of payments (£m)	Total official financing (£m)
1966	30,380	90.4	104	591
1967	31,983	92.5	−300	671
1968	34,146	95.9	−287	1410
1969	35,937	97.8	440	−687
1970	39,487	100.0	695	−1420
1971	44,574	102.1	1058	−3271
1972	46,679	105.3	105	1141
1973	57,915	111.7	−922	771
1974	66,574	110.8	−3565	1646
1975	83,060	109.1	−1701	1465
1976	96,676	111.5	−1405	3628

Source: Annual Abstract of Statistics

Index